BRADY

Being a Medical Transcriptionist

Brady Medical Clerical Series

Kay Cox, Series Editor

Jacquelyn Marshall and Kathleen Harris
Being a Medical Clerical Worker: An Introductory Core Text

Kathy McMiller
Being a Medical Records Clerk

Linda Barber
Being a Medical Admitting Clerk

Linda Barber and Donna Lee Derbish
Being a Medical Insurance Clerk

Norma Lee Morrow
Being a Medical Transcriptionist

Laurie Dodson
Being a Medical Information Coder

BRADY

Being a Medical Transcriptionist

NORMA LEE MORROW, CMA-C
Southern California College of Medical and Dental Assistants

BRADY
PRENTICE HALL CAREER & TECHNOLOGY
Englewood Cliffs, New Jersey 07632

Library of Congress Cataloging-in-Publication Data

Morrow, Norma Lee, (date)
Being a medical transcriptionist / Norma Lee Morrow
p. cm. — (Brady medical clerical series)
Includes bibliographical references and index
ISBN 0-89303-082-1
1. Medical transcription. I. Series.
[DNLM: 1. Medical Records. 2. Medical Secretaries.
3. Nomenclature. W 80 M983b]
R728.8.M67 1992
653'.18—dc20
DNLM/DLC
for Library of Congress 91-34181
CIP

Acquisition Editor: Mark Hartman
Editorial Assistant: Elizabeth O'Brien
Cover Photograph: George Dodson
Prepress Buyer: Ilene Levy
Manufacturing Buyer: Ed O'Dougherty
Production Editor: Patrick Walsh

A Simon & Schuster Company
Englewood Cliffs, New Jersey 07632

Printed in the United States of America
10 9 8 7 6 5

ISBN 0-89303-082-1

Prentice-Hall International (UK), *London*
Prentice-Hall of Australia Pty. Limited, *Sydney*
Prentice-Hall Canada Inc., *Toronto*
Prentice-Hall Hispanoamericana, S.A., *Mexico*
Prentice-Hall of India Private Limited, *New Delhi*
Prentice-Hall of Japan, Inc., *Tokyo*
Simon & Schuster Asia Pte. Ltd., *Singapore*
Editora Prentice-Hall do Brasil, Ltda., *Rio de Janeiro*

To All Former Students
This is lovingly dedicated

Contents

Chapter 6 Numbers 65

Chapter 7 Sentence Structure 73

Chapter 8 Proofreading 79

Chapter 9 Letter Writing 87

Chapter 10 Medical Terminology Review 99

Foreword

There are abundant career opportunities for medical clerical workers. In fact, the U.S. Bureau of Labor Statistics has placed medical offices and health care facilities among the top ten industries expected to generate the largest number of new jobs to the year 2000. Ninety percent growth is projected for medical assistants and 75 percent growth for medical records technicians alone. The reason for this staggering increase in demand for medical clerical workers is the aging of America and the enormous amount of resultant paperwork. One of the largest jobs in the health care industry will be maintaining those medical records. Legal considerations, insurance billing, and Medicare have made the proper management of patients' charts increasingly important.

Industry, on the other hand, reports that there are not nearly enough trained medical clerical workers to meet the demand and many jobs go unfilled. Adequate training opportunities and training tools are in short supply, particulary in some career areas.

The Brady Medical Clerical Series was created in recognition of these needs. Designed as easy-to-understand yet comprehensive texts, this series guides students through the duties and responsibilities of medical clerical workers in their chosen fields. *Being a Medical Clerical Worker: An Introductory Core Text* contains information considered common to all medical clerical areas. This book, *Being a Medical Transcriptionist*, is one in a series for students interested in working in medical transcribing.

It is hoped that this new series will make a significant contribution toward filling the gap of supply and demand for medical clerical works and that you, the student, will utilize these books to the fullest degree as you embark on your new career.

Kay Cox
Series Editor

ABOUT THE SERIES EDITOR

Kay Cox, R.N., M.A., Series Editor, conceived and coordinated this project. She is a Health Careers Specialist; Assistant Professor of Medical Assisting at Saddleback College; instructor of Medical Assisting and Health Unit Coordinators at the Capistrano-Laguna Beach Regional Occupational Program in California and author of Brady's *Being a Health Unit Coordinator.*

ABOUT THE AUTHOR

Norma Lee Morrow, CMA-C, CCMA-AC, author, began teaching nights at Southern California College of Medical Assistants after 17 years in the medical field. In 1970 she created the Medical Assistant Program for the Garden Grove Unified School District. Additional courses of Transcription and Insurance were added in 1973. For 21 years she has coordinated the program and taught all phases of medical assisting at the following schools: Santiago High School, Lincoln Educational Traning Center, and Chapman-Hettinga Educational Center. For ten of those years she has also been associated with Central County Regional Occupational Program of Orange County, California, and for two of those years she also served as Health Careers Resource Teacher for the district.

Preface

This text has grown, like Topsy, from a very small beginning to its present form. It all began many years ago when I searched for material to begin a medical transcription class, because some of our students were interested. The introduction they received in medical assisting served to "whet the appetite" to learn more. For years there were only a handful who were taught in an individually self-paced class, as an adjunct to my other classes.

Over the years both the interest and number of students have grown. A few years ago, there were so many students that a separate class was formed. Most of the material contained herein has been used and tested by numbers of students over the years. These lessons on punctuation, capitalization, grammar, and the like have been used in conjunction with a couple of sets of tapes which I made over a period of time. A recent addition is a set of tapes made by doctors from many foreign countries.

It was never my intention to write a book. I intended only to teach interested students the basics to fit them for entry-level jobs as transcriptionists. Without exception, those who finished the course, over the years, obtained jobs.

This text can be used to teach beginning transcriptionists in any setting: clinic, acute or convalescent hospital, doctor's office, or laboratory. It should be used along with tapes of actual cases, in addition to the Learning Activities included.

Each chapter has objectives so that the student will know what is expected, and Learning Activities to aid in accomplishing those objectives. There is an instructor's manual with answers and suggestions for other life-like situations for learning.

ACKNOWLEDGMENTS

This was written at the same time that I was teaching 38–40 hours weekly, plus preparation and grading time, teaching an adult Bible class, helping "parent" an 87-year-old father, and also during the loss of two sisters. I had no time to seek outside encouragement or collaboration, so it would probably not have been done except for the following:

The summer class of 1989, who helped me find and correct errors.

My daughter, Sharilyn Lee Bell, who read manuscripts and told me, faithfully, when they were too wordy.

Kay Cox, R.N., instructor, author, series editor, who edited and patiently encouraged me during the most difficult times.

Other Encouragers

Loree De Bonis Cox, C.M.A., instructor and friend.

Glenn Crawford, R.O.P., administrator and friend.

Beverly Schmidt, former student and friend, who was always there to help with the typing, at many odd and inconvenient times. She has my everlasting thanks.

Others who inspired me but who perhaps never realized it: Corinne Soltif, Department Administrator of Records at Kaiser, Anaheim; Mary Kinn, C.P.A., instructor, author, and friend; Marilyn T. Fordney, instructor, author, and speaker; and Veronica Walker, instructor and friend, who originally introduced me to word processing.

Norma Lee Morrow

CHAPTER 1

Introduction to Being a Medical Transcriptionist

OBJECTIVES

After completing this chapter, through performing the learning activities, the student should be able, with 100 percent accuracy, to:

1. Identify the traits and skills necessary to be a transcriptionist.
2. Understand the importance of medical records and the ethics involved.
3. Explain why an understanding of medical terminology and anatomical terms is important.
4. Understand why speed, as well as accuracy, is needed.
5. Assemble a transcriptionist's notebook or reference file list and learn terms pertaining to the career.
6. Know the places where transcriptionists can work.
7. Find information for the handicapped student.
8. Understand the circumstances for release of information and the importance of subpoenas.
9. Distinguish between medical records and medical reports.
10. Know where to obtain information on references and other material helpful to a handicapped transcriptionist.
11. Explain how a transcriptionist may become certified.

12. Define terms listed for this chapter.
13. Explain how transcriptionists stay abreast of changes.

KEY TERMS

HMO Health Maintenance Organization
PPO Preferred Provider Organization
Voc. Rehab. Vocational Rehabilitation
AAMT American Association for Medical Transcriptionists
AHA American Heart Association, American Hospital Association
VIMT Visually Impaired Medical Transcriptionist
CMT Certified Medical Transcriptionist
CEC Continuing Education Credits
AMA American Medical Association

Welcome to a fascinating, extremely necessary, and frequently intriguing vocation. Having chosen medical transcription as a career, you need to understand some of the traits and skills that will be necessary for you to have.

KEY IDEA: SKILLS

Medical transcriptionists need good typing skills. Both speed and accuracy are required: speed, because records need to be available in written form as soon as possible; accuracy, because spelling is vital to understanding and correctly filing medical records. Terminology, including anatomical words, is also vitally important to keep the flow of work smooth and continuous. A good knowledge of English grammar, spelling, and proofreading abilities are also necessary. The knowledge of medical and surgical terms and drug and laboratory language is essential. Any experience in the medical field is helpful. The more experience you have had in the medical field, the easier the transition to medical transcription may be. It is not unusual to move up the career ladder from medical secretary or medical transcriptionist to transcriptionist.

KEY IDEA: TRAITS NEEDED

Even though the transcriptionist is an essential part of the medical team, for the most part you will work alone. You must like to work independently of others. You must have initiative, be dependable (always be there), have an intelligent and inquisitive mind, and have a desire to turn out attractive and accurate copies. No half-measures ever! You must be as dedicated to your job as the doctor or any other member of the team.

KEY IDEA: IMPORTANCE OF RECORDS

The best medical care can be provided only if medical records are accurate and complete. Medical records are almost as old as man. Records have been found in excavations that go back many centuries. The Greeks and early Romans have contributed much to the keeping of medical records. The patient's record has been and remains a means of communication with utmost importance to the proper delivery of medical care.

Technically, you could say transcription began with early scribes who faithfully recorded what was dictated to them. Over many centuries, secretaries, steno pad notebook in hand, became the transcriptionists of their day. Gradually machines have almost replaced them. It became easier to speak into a machine or telephone, which was always handy. As the importance of complete records grew, so did the specialty.

KEY IDEA: ACCURACY

Reliance on accurate medical records continues to increase due to tremendous technical and scientific advances and the development of more medico-legal problems. In addition to aiding in delivery of the best care possible, accurate records are extremely important to help avoid those problems. Important information for research purposes, including disease statistics, is also gleaned from good records. Attorneys, other doctors, employers, insurance companies, hospitals, and courts may require copies of records; they *must be* correct.

KEY IDEA: SPEED

While you strive to be correct, you must also work on speed. With the 15-minute tape (dictated by the doctor) averaging 150 lines, and the 30-minute tape containing 300 to 400 lines, speed is next to accuracy in importance. Expected output is anywhere from 100 lines per hour to 1300 lines per eight-hour day. This estimate has some variables, according to the place of employment, type of equipment being used, and the type of dictator. In an area with many foreign accents, your production expectation may be lessened somewhat. (Check appendix for helpful hints on pronunciation.)

KEY IDEA: WHERE YOU CAN WORK

Often when you think of transcription, you automatically picture an acute-care hospital. That is only the beginning of the career opportunities. Employers are many and varied: Research centers, convalescent hospitals, individual doctors, group practice, HMOs, PPOs, private and public health centers, and lawyers whose specialties are medical litigation all require the services of a transcriptionist. There is always the possibility of becoming your own employer, serving clients out of your home. Both part-time and full-time jobs are available, but if you work on your own, you can set up your own hours. For some people, that is a great advantage. It can also be very lucrative.

KEY IDEA: POSSIBILITIES FOR THE PHYSICALLY CHALLENGED

There is opportunity in the field of transcription for various physically challenged personnel. Digital dexterity (dextrous use of the fingers) is necessary at this point, but it may change with voice-activated equipment. The visually impaired have more than a few possibilities. Textbooks in braille or on cassette make it feasible to learn the theory involved. For the blind, or nearly blind, there are many sources of assistance. Some examples are state Departments of Vocational Rehabilitation, Braille Institute, American Heart Association, American Association for Medical Transcriptionists, Visually Impaired Medical Transcriptionists, Easter Seal program, and Community Chest.

KEY IDEA: UPGRADING

If you wish to excel, keep up with all the latest information and equipment by becoming a part of a professional organization. You may want to join the American Association for Medical Transcriptionists. After three years of hospital transcription, you may take their certification examination. A Certified Medical Transcriptionist (CMT) participates in an ongoing educa-

tion program. CMTs are required to obtain 30 continuing education credits (CEC) every three years.

If you desire more information, contact:

American Association for Medical Transcription
P.O. Box 6187
Modesto, California 95355

KEY IDEA: ETHICAL AND LEGAL RESPONSIBILITIES

Basically, the ethical and legal responsibilities are the same for a medical transcriptionist as they are for all medical and paramedical personnel. See the core textbook, *Being a Medical Clerk*. The AAMT adopted its code of ethics in 1979. See Exhibit 1-1.

It is your responsibility to protect and guard any records that pass through your hands. Medical records are the property of the institution or physician where they originate. Regardless of who requests a copy, you are never to release any copy or information without the proper written consent of the patient and permission of the owner of the records. However, some correspondence or social service records may not be considered to be part of the medical record. If you have any question concerning the release of information, even with a court subpoena (a written legal order directing a person to appear in court to give testimony, show specified records, and so on), check with your immediate supervisor before copying or releasing it. (See Exhibit 1-2.)

Code of Ethics
of the
American Assocation for Medical Transcription

1. Be aware that is by our standards of conduct and professionalism that the entire Association is evaluated, for the conduct of one individual can be the vertex upon which the future of the Association may depend.
2. Conduct ourselves in the practice of our profession as to bring dignity and honor to ourselves, the profession of medical transcription, and the American Association for Medical Transcription.
3. Place the goals and purposes of the Association above greed, personal gain, and interpersonal relationships by discouraging dissension and by working for the good of the majority.
4. Refuse to participate in or conceal unethical procedures or practices in relationships with other associations or individuals.
5. Recognize the source of authority and powers delegated to us as individuals and observe the limitations and confinements of said authority and power.
6. Discharge honorably the responsibility of any Association positions to which we are elected or appointed.
7. Preserve the confidential nature of professional judgments and determinations made by the official committees of the Association.
8. Represent truthfully and accurately all professional committees in any official transaction whether that transaction be within the Association or in the form of representation of ourselves as members of the Association.
9. Protect the privacy and confidentially of the individual medical record to avoid disclosure of personally identifiable medical and social information and professional medical judgments.
10. Srtive to increase the body of systematic knowledge and individual competence of the medical transcription profession through continued self-improvement and the constructive exchange of knowledge and concepts with others in our profession.
11. Uphold the standards of and safeguard the profession of medical transcription by reporting in writing to the Code of Ethics Committee any breach of this Code of Ethics by any fellow member of the medical transcription profession.

Adopted, September 1979

Exhibit 1-1. (Used by permission of the American Association for Medical Transcription.)

Form D-1

AUTHORIZATION FOR DISCLOSURE OF INFORMATION BY PATIENT'S PHYSICIAN

1. I authorize Dr. ____________________to disclose complete information to ____________________ concerning his medical findings and treatment of the undersigned from on or about ____________________ 19 ______ until date of the conclusion of such treatment.

2. Further, I authorize him to testify, without limitation, as to all of his medical findings and the treatment administered to the undersigned, in any legal action, suit, or proceedings to which I am, or may become, a party; and I waive on behalf of myself and any other persons who may have an interest in the matter, all provisions of law relating to the disclosure of confidential medical information.

Signed ________________________
Place ________________________
Date ________________________

Witness ________________________

Exhibit 1-2. (*Source: Medicolegal forms with Legal Analysis*, 3rd. ed., Office of the General Counsel, 1973.)

The person who serves the subpoena is given an amount of money (basic + mileage) to be given to the recipient of the subpoena. If you ever receive a subpoena, personally or for your employer, ask for the *serving fee* to make the transaction complete. Even when a legal photocopier comes to make records, the same rules apply. Ask for a fee, based on the size of the record to be copied. These fees are to reimburse the employer for the clerical time involved. In addition, the records should all be numbered by page, or someone should observe while the records are being copied.

KEY IDEA: CORRECTIONS

In another chapter (see page 147), corrections will be discussed in detail. If, however, it becomes necessary to retype a report because of many typing errors, there is a specific way to handle this. The second draft should be made. Write on it "corrected for typing errors," and then include both the original and the second copy stapled together, with the corrected one on top. The physician or administrator should sign both copies. In the event of legal action, the original will give evidence that the report was sent out as soon as possible following treatment.

KEY IDEA: KINDS OF REPORTS AND MEDICAL RECORDS

You will be typing numerous kinds of medical reports and records. What is the difference between the two? A *medical record* is the authentication of facts and events that have happened to a patient. A *medical report* is the result of an investigation and is a permanent legal document.

Some examples of medical reports are lab reports or tests, radiology reports, histories and physical examinations for admitting to the hospital, consultations or examinations by specialists, operative reports, daily progress notes, admitting and discharge sheets, CT scans, pathology reports, and the like.

Medical reports might be used by attorneys, insurance companies, government agencies, or for statistical purposes. Tapes used in conjunction with this text will have you transcribing some of these. Sample medical reports are seen on pages 123 to 146.

A *medical record* is information set down to authenticate evidence of facts and events concerning the patient's treatment. Medical records legally belong to the physician or institution involved in patient care. As such, the physician or institution is legally and ethically responsible to protect them. These records are for three main purposes:

1. Health-care purposes: To aid in the diagnosis and treatment of the patient by providing information to all medical personnel.
2. Research purposes: To provide statistical information for the advancement of science and medicine.
3. Legal purposes: To comply with the law and aid in support of a claim.

Medical records should be completed promptly to prevent omissions or errors. It is most important that the transcriptionist enter only accurate material in order to help avoid an expensive legal suit.

Both *privileged information* and *nonprivileged information* are contained in the *medical record*. *Privileged information* is directly related to the treatment and progress of the patient. It can be given out *only* with the written authorization of the patient. The one exception is information required by law to be reported to the Health Department or other law enforcement agency. The transcriptionist would seldom, if ever, be involved with that.

Nonprivileged information is not related to the treatment of the patient. It involves the following:

1. Dates of treatment, admission, and discharge.
2. The number of times and dates of treatment and whether the patient was ill or operated on.
3. The complete name of the patient and the address at the time of admission to the hospital.
4. Name of relative or friend given when first seen or admitted.

As stated previously, if you have any questions as to what is permissible, check with your superior.

KEY IDEA: YOUR PERSONAL FILE

Every aspiring transcriptionist should begin a personal file of learning from the first day. Included in that file or notebook will be a list of medical or anatomical terms, names of medications, sound-alike terms, abbreviations, references or agencies, and *any word or fact* that you have to look up. This can be done with 3 × 5-in. index cards, kept alphabetically, or in 8-1/2 × 11-in., three-ring notebook. The notebook or cards should be alphabetized and added to consistently. This will become an invaluable tool to you in your transcription career. In one notebook, you bring together the knowledge gained from many sources. Besides, it is always easier to find information you have used and recorded than to stop and look it up in another source *again.*

A notebook is usually preferred over a large card file because it is easier to refer to and transport. A Rolodex card file, which is compact and can be added to easily, is another efficient tool.

SUMMARY

A career as a medical transcriptionist can be exciting and fulfilling. You must be dedicated, must be a self-starter, must have initiative, and must be willing to work alone most of the time. You need to be accurate and attain a better than average speed. Attention to detail, adherence to the legal and ethical aspects of medical records, and an ongoing desire to learn will help you develop your career in medical transcription.

LEARNING ACTIVITIES

ACTIVITY 1-1

Fill in the blanks.

1. Explain the difference between:

a. A medical record ______________________________

____

b. A medical report ______________________________

____

2. Write out the definition for each of the following abbreviations:

a. AAMT ______________________________

b. AHA (both) ______________________________

(and) ______________________________

c. AMA ______________________________

d. CEC ______________________________

e. CMT ______________________________

f. HMO ______________________________

g. PPO ______________________________

h. VIMT ______________________________

i. Voc. Rehab. ______________________________

3. Give three reasons why medical records are important.

a. ______________________________

b. ______________________________

c. ______________________________

4. List ten prospective places of employment as a transcriptionist.

a. ______________________________

b. ______________________________

c. ______________________________

d. ______________________________

e. ______________________________

f. ______________________________

g. ______________________________

h. ______________________________

i. ______________________________

j. ______________________________

5. You can find information for the handicapped student by contacting ______________________________
or ______________________________

6. You can become certified after ____ years of hospital transcribing. The examination for certifictation is given by
____

7. What is one way to stay abreast of the latest in equipment and transcribing information? ______________________________
____

8. Explain why terminology of medicine and anatomy are important in this career. ______________________________
____

9. No information or copies should ever be released without
____

10. Why is a subpoena different from an ordinary request for records? ______________________________

11. Name six skills and/or traits needed to become a transcriptionist:
    a. ______________________________
    b. ______________________________
    c. ______________________________
    d. ______________________________
    e. ______________________________
    f. ______________________________

ACTIVITY 1-2

Obtain a three-holed, 8-½ × 11-in. or 9-½ × 6-in. notebook and alphabetical (A–Z) index guides. Begin your first entries with the abbreviations from this chapter. Add any word or term you have to look up.

NOTES

CHAPTER 2

Know Your Equipment

OBJECTIVES

Following the reading of this chapter a student should be able, through written or oral testing, with a 90 percent accuracy, to:

1. Understand the operation of commonly used transcription/dictation equipment.
2. Define vocabulary terms from this chapter.
3. Identify different types of typewriters and transcribing equipment, including accessory equipment.
4. Understand how copying machines can be used in the transcribing process.
5. Explain equipment used for the handicapped.
6. Understand transcribing terms and how to prepare for transcribing.
7. Explain why word processing features are helpful in transcription.
8. Be able to demonstrate the knowledge of the equipment available to the satisfaction of the teacher.
9. Identify the greatest enemy of all (or any) equipment.

KEY TERMS

The use of transcription equipment necessitates the knowledge of some key phrases or terms. The list given below is common to most equipment.

Adaptor a device for connecting two parts of an apparatus not ordinarily connected.

Audio any device that produces sound.

Auto Backspace built-in control that allows automatic repeating of a word or words.

Batch similar documents collected for memory in groups.

Bit smallest unit of information recognized by a computer.

Byte a given number of bits known as a unit of computer storage.

Cassette magnetic tape wound on two reels and encased in a plastic or metal container. It is used to mount or insert into a playback device.

Cassette Tape a magnetic tape wound on two reels, encased in a plastic or metal container, inserted in a playback device.

Cassette Compartment small opening into which cassette is placed with tape side number 1 up.

Clear control that clears the display for dictation and resets to zero; sometimes called a *reset.*

Command Key the key used to enter a specified command into word processing equipment.

CRT display terminal, similar to a television screen, attached to word processing equipment.

Cursor a lighted, or blinking, indicator on a CRT screen. It indicates the place for entering new text or correcting same.

Daisywheel a flat disk with the keyboard characters around the circumference. A *print wheel.*

Delete a command to remove a specific part of the text in word processing.

Dictation that which has been spoken and recorded on the tape cassette.

Dictation Display lighted area that shows how many minutes have been used by the person dictating or transcribing.

Disc (or Disk) magnetic storage device; it can be made of flexible plastic (floppy disc) or rigid material (hard disc).

Display the text that appears on the screen *or* a command to produce a specific text on the CRT.

Dual Pitch that element allowing a typewriter to type either pica, elite, or 15-pitch.

Editing to revise or correct text.

Eject Button the control to open the cassette door.

Element component, similar to a golf ball, used to print the keyboard characters on some electric typewriters.

Elite typewriter type, measuring 12 characters per linear inch.

Fast Forward the control that winds tape forward quickly without sending sound through the speaker.

Font type of one size and style.

Foot Control pedal used to activate tape play by pressing down on it with the foot.

Global Change using one instruction in a word processing system; the ability to change a word or portion of text everywhere it appears with only one instruction.

Hard Copy a document; written, typed, or printed copy.

Hardware the physical components of a computer system.

Headset usually U-shaped band device fitting over the head or under the chin and having a hearing device for each ear.

Index Counter a fast forward.

Input information to be entered into a system for processing.

Insert word processing function that allows new material to be inserted.

Justification a character spacing adjustment that allows the right margin to be produced as evenly as the left.

Keyboarding like typing, except that it includes the extra instruction keys of a word processing machine.

Medium (plural Media) material on which information is recorded.

Memory that section of a computer where instructions, data, and information are stored to be retrieved at a later date.

Memory Typewriter a typewriter with smaller, more limited amount of the above capacity.

Menu a list of previously stored items displayed on a CRT screen from which the typist can choose the word processing document to be edited. Also, a list of functions to be performed.

Microcassette miniature cassette tape that fits into small hand-held transcribing unit.

Microphone used for transmitting or recording speech or music— usually a hand-held device.

Modem acronym for MOdulator DEModulator unit; a device that converts data into signals for telephone transmission, and at the other end, back again into data.

Output recorded information that is processed, revised, and printed out (the printout).

Pica typewriter type, larger than elite, measuring 10 characters per linear inch.

Platen the roller against which the keys strike.

Playback the control that allows recorded material to be heard; usually this control is on the foot pedal.

Program software.

RAM random access memory.

Retrieve to find stored information.

Rewind control that reverses cassette tape for replay.

Scan control that rewinds the cassette and generates transcription display.

Scroll ability to move the text horizontally or vertically and to flip document pages on a CRT.

Software programs or instruction used to support a piece of equipment.

Speaker built-in amplifier that allows playback to be heard through attached earphones.

Transcription conversion of recorded dictation to hard copy.

Voice Activation ability of a machine to recognize and respond to spoken words.

Warranty a written statement giving a time period in which the manufacturer will be responsible for repairing or replacing equipment.

Word Processing a method of printed communications that helps facilitate the flow of related office work.

INTRODUCTION

Numerous types of equipment are used for transcription. Some are very basic or fundamental. Some are very sophisticated. It is exciting to think what technology may develop for the future.

KEY IDEA: TYPEWRITERS

Typewriters are an example of the basic equipment available. There are three types: manual, electric, and electronic or memory. Hospitals' and physicians' offices will most often use the electric or electronic because their capabilities are more varied. They are extremely efficient, and the typed material has a better appearance.

Manual Typewriters

The manual typewriter can perform all the necessary basic functions, but everything, including the carriage return, is

performed manually. It is, therefore, slower than the electric or electronic. It will have only one kind of type, either elite or pica.

Electric Typewriters

The electric typewriter can have either a moveable or immovable carriage, and interchangeable typing elements. You can even type in script. Where the basic typewriter has either pica or elite type, the electric can have both. It is called *dual pitch.* Elite is especially good to use when space is limited, especialy with insurance forms. Pica is better used for letter writing or reports. When space is at a premium, the typewriter with an immoveable carriage is a good choice. Some typewriters come with three choices, the third being a 15-character-per-inch size. This is especially helpful for use with small areas on forms. All of these typewriters have interchangeable elements or daisy wheels to vary print appearance with different fonts.

Electronic Typewriters

The capabilities of the electronic typewriter are many. It has single-element typing technology, combined with memory, so it will perform many tasks automatically that would ordinarily have to be done manually. It will center, underscore, indent, store phrases, and do automatic error correction, all from memory. Other special features include margins and tabs, number alignment, proportional spacing, automatic carriage return, column layout, bold type, and display typing. These special features are explained and demonstrated in their accompanying manuals. Many also have the capability of making the right margin as even as the left, through adjustment of spacing. When multiple copies of form letters or reports are needed, the memory will handle it. Manufacturers can upgrade many of these to have extra storage capacity, or an external storage medium.

KEY IDEA: MAINTENANCE AND ACCESSORIES

The enemy of all machines is dust. Because you want your typewriter to function well and turn out professional-looking work, you should always be careful to turn it off and cover it whenever it is not in use. One exception: some memory typewriters lose memory when you turn them off. Although some equipment does not need to be unplugged, every part of it needs to be kept dust free. Both the typing characters and the body can be cleaned with a slightly dampened cloth. No abrasives should ever be used, but typing characters can also be cleaned on a regular basis with a brush and typecleaning fluid. Do not ever erase over a typewriter. The eraser "dust" clogs moving parts and can harm equipment. If your machine does not have a correction key, use correction tape that lifts off or covers over the error. You can then make your correction.

The condition of your equipment affects your finished product. Your equipment manual has numerous tips for maintenance or repair. When a problem arises and a repairman seems necessary, troubleshoot first. Your manual has suggestions on what to do. When you have checked everything possible, only then make a call for repair.

Perhaps you never thought of a chair as an accessory to a typewriter, but it is. The chair should be one that will adjust to the individual's height and build. The table where the typewriter sits should be of proper height. This will reduce fatigue and aid in the typist's productivity. Lighting should be adequate. Eye strain and neck- and backaches can be minimized by the use of an electronic copyholder. For a person who is shorter than the average, a small footstool will reduce or avoid back problems. Proper posture should be maintained at all times.

Ribbons and correction ribbons should be the ones recommended by the manufacturer. A cheap ribbon may dirty your keys and machine. If it is not the recommended one, your correction key may not work. Many typewriters have the snap-in/snap-out cartridge, which is not only convenient but also keeps the hands clean.

The stenographer's pad and pencil have now been replaced in many offices by electronic dictation and transcription systems, some of which include computers. (Courtesy of Philips Business Systems, a Division of North American Phillips Corporation.)

KEY IDEA: CHANGING TRANSCRIPTION EQUIPMENT

Technology for processing, storing, and communicating information is rapidly changing. Much less time is spent on routine tasks and efficiency is greater. The need for shorthand is almost nonexistent, but dictation and transcription skills are still very much in demand. A recent survey indicates that 60 percent of all offices now use dictation and transcription on word processors. This figure may soon increase to 100 percent, according to some current secretarial handbooks.

Machine dictation provides more flexibility than an "in-person" dictation system. The secretary does not need to be

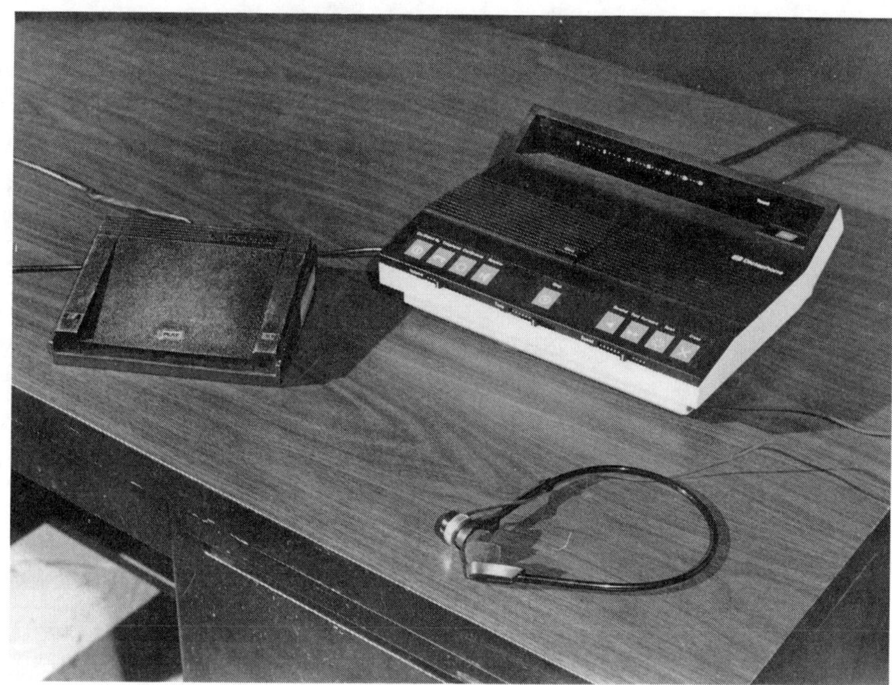

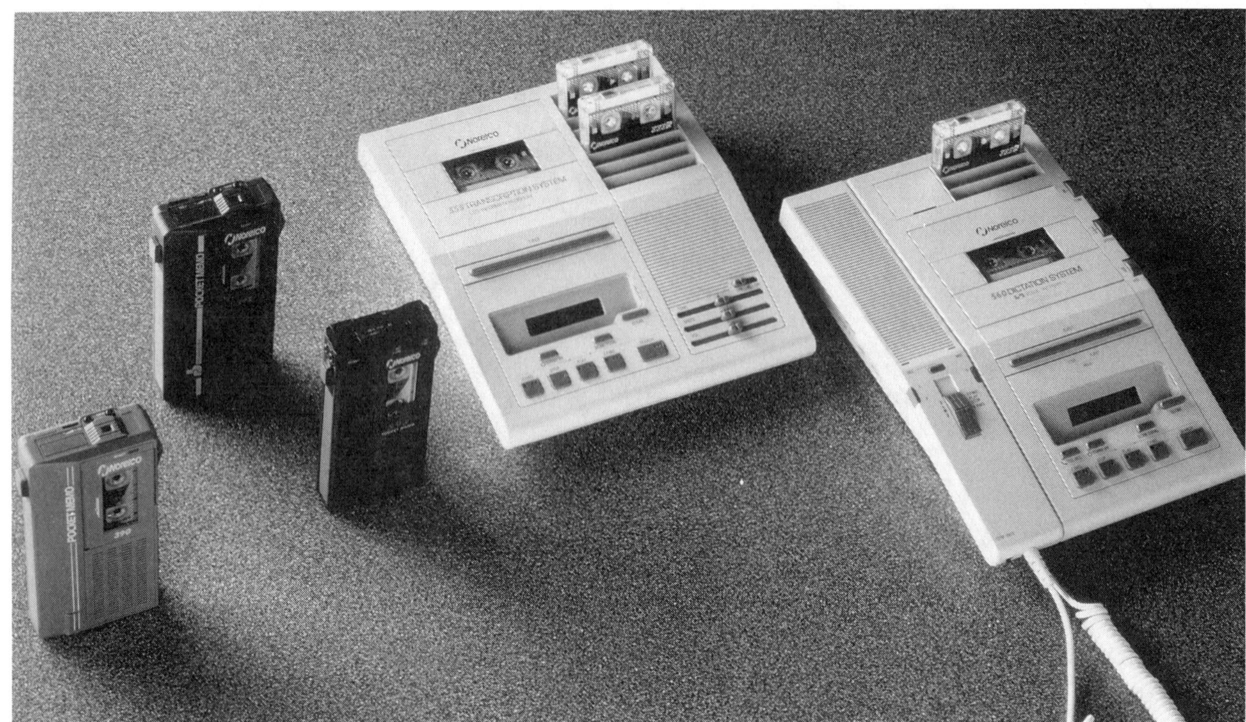

These hand-held dictation machines (left), desktop transcription machine (center), and desktop dictation machine (right) all use the same size tape cassette. (Courtesy of Philips Business Systems, a Division of North American Phillips Corporation.)

present. Dictation can be done while commuting, on a business trip, or at home, as well as at the office.

KEY IDEA: DESKTOP MODELS

When a *desktop dictation machine* is standard in an office, it usually consists of two to three pieces of equipment:

1. For dictating only: a dictation unit.
2. For the secretary to transcribe the dictation: a transcription unit, which includes headphones and foot pedals.
3. For both dictation and transcription: a combination unit.
4. For final printout or record: a typewriter or word processor.

KEY IDEA: PORTABLE EQUIPMENT

The variety of *portable dictation equipment* is exciting. Small, lightweight, portable, hand-held machines are produced by many companies. They operate on either wall plug or batteries, produce good-quality material, and record on cassettes, minicassettes, and microcassettes. Some machines have the capability of using either one of two sizes. They can be used anywhere: the morning walk, in the car, at meetings or con-

Portable (hand-held) dictation machines. (left, courtesy of Philips Business Systems, a Division of North American Phillips Corporation; right, courtesy of Radio Shack, a Division of Tandy Corporation)

ventions. Transcribing units are also made to handle more than one size of cassette.

KEY IDEA: TELECOMMUNICATIONS

Doctors *dictate by phone* by dialing a special number that seizes the transcribing equipment. This can be set up with a rather large variety of transcribing equipment. Many doctors find it more comfortable to talk over the phone rather than into a recorder. They can call from a phone anywhere into the hospital or office that has this equipment.

KEY IDEA: TANK-TYPE MACHINES

Tank-type machines receive direct input from one or more dictating stations that use telephone-type services. The transcribing unit may be located in a basement or other out-of-the way place in a hospital or word processing department. The transcriptionist does not physically transfer or handle the recorded medium from the machine. Manual controls and the foot pedal on the transcribing unit are the only things that the transcriptionist uses from the receiving unit.

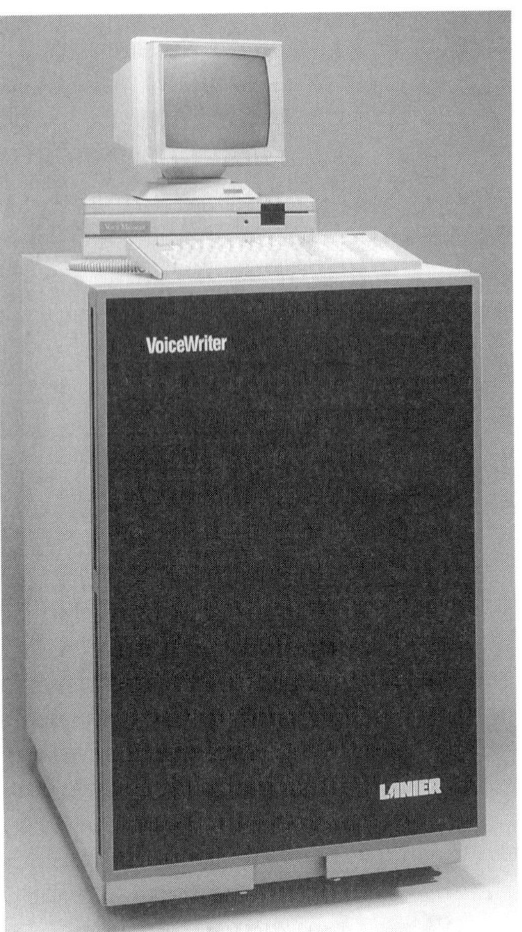

Large computerized systems provide centrally located storage that can serve many dictators and transcriptionists. (Courtesy of Lanier Voice Products)

KEY IDEA: CASSETTE-CHANGER CENTRAL RECORDER

This *central recorder* may hold 15 to 25 cassettes, programmed to be changed automatically by one of two methods: (1) the number of dictators who have access, or (2) the percentage of tape used. In either case it can be set up for each person's dictation to be on a separate cassette.

Alphascribe, a company in San Diego, has carried this one step farther through voice-activated recording that is simultaneously recorded on a cassette. Transcriptionists then use the cassettes to record or print out the material.

KEY IDEA: TYPES OF MEDIA

Magnetic discs, tapes, or cassettes are used as media in an almost limitless variety of machines. All of the above allow the dictator to correct errors at the time of dictation. You can record 15 to 90 minutes of dictation on each side of standard, micro-, or minicassettes. They can be erased and reused or taped over. Some machines are equipped with a minicassette adaptor, allowing you to use either the standard or the minicassette.

An embossing medium is also available. It records sounds on grooves pressed by a stylus onto the surface. A disadvantage is that they cannot be erased, so they can be used only one time. Since they cannot be erased, errors have to be corrected later, with the dictator indicating where the correction is to be made. One advantage is that they are inexpensive and can be stored for a permanent record.

Regardless of the media, most equipment follows the same basic transcribing procedure. One thing that should be considered when buying new equipment is voice fidelity. Ask for a sample recording to which you can listen. Most machines are equipped with a warning tone toward the end of the tape, and some warn you if a tape is broken.

KEY IDEA: USING THE MACHINE

The foot pedal is the control you must master. When you put pressure on the pedal, the machine starts. When you want to stop, simply lift your foot. You may fast forward, return for a few words, or rewind as far as you wish, all with the foot pedal control. Some automatically repeat a few words every time you begin listening again. Some equipment also has a hand control placed close to the space bar of the keyboard.

Hearing is through earphones plugged into the machine. You listen to as much as you can retain, type, and continue listening. Speed can be adjusted from quite slow to faster than normal speech. You will usually begin with the speed a little slower than normal. Eventually you will be able to adjust your speed of typing and listening so that they will coincide. At that point you will be typing and listening at the same time and speed. Your skill in doing this will gradually increase; so will your typing speed.

Most machines have some type of indicator to let you know where you are on the tape. These indicators can show either seconds or minutes used, and are reset at the beginning of each tape. If you learn to rely on that indication feature, you may save time by beginning at the same place, even though someone else has used the tape since you did. Record the amount of time into the tape and begin at the same spot the next time you use it.

KEY IDEA: DICTATION

All transcriptionists should try dictating. In so doing, they will gain knowledge of the problems encountered by the dictator. This may help you to aid your employer by making suggestions. You might say:

> I would like to type your material as speedily and efficiently as possible. It would help me to do that if you would (for example) indicate periods or other punctuation and capitalization where needed. Also, I am sometimes uncertain when to begin a new paragraph. It would be especially helpful if you could so indicate.

As stated elsewhere, some employers expect you to have the skills necessary to punctuate and paragraph without direction. Nevertheless, after you have tried dictation for a few times and then listened to yourself, you will be more sympathetic to the dictator's problems.

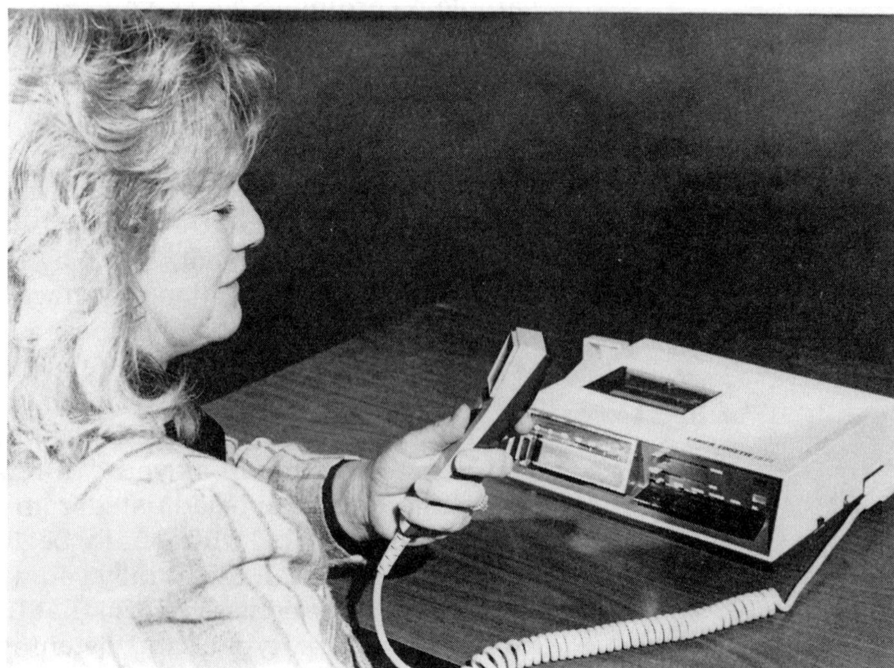

Be certain always to let your boss know you appreciate good dictating. Also, remember to return the dictating equipment to the ready position with fresh tape (or media) inserted. In that way your employer can dictate immediately without having to set up.

Before you try dictating, make a list of all the problems you encounter in transcribing and be aware of them as you go.

1. State what you are dictating and what size and specific type of paper you wish to be used.
2. Give the name of the person to whom it is directed; also the address and ZIP code.
3. Spell any difficult names or words as you go.
4. State the number of copies desired.
5. State when a new paragraph begins by saying, "period paragraph." In dictating paragraphs notes would be helpful.
6. If you are dictating data to be filled in on a form, it is best to have a copy in front of you.
7. Indicate punctuation, such as commas, hyphens, parentheses, quotation marks (quotes), plurals, or capitalization that would not ordinarily be done.
8. Speak distinctly and fairly slowly. Do not eat or drink as you talk. If you must pause and think, shut off the recorder, thus eliminating "uh," "um," and the like.

KEY IDEA: EQUIPMENT FOR THE PHYSICALLY CHALLENGED

Many improvements and adaptations in the usual transcribing equipment have made it easier for the physically challenged person. For persons with lower limb handicaps, adaptations can be made. Instead of using the traditional foot pedal, they could start or stop a machine with the hands, or in some instances use the voice as an activator. If a person is forced by a handicap to sit for long hours, a job as a transcriptionist could be a welcome career.

For the blind or visually impaired, numerous methods have been developed to help them function as medical secretaries or transcriptionists.

For the partially sighted, a video magnifier can make it possible to produce perfect copies. This system has a moveable stand with a high-powered lens focused on it. A small-to-medium-sized closed circuit television screen magnifies and enlarges the material on that stand. The typist can enlarge the copy on the stand to whatever size is suitable for his or her visual needs. The screen can be changed from a black background with white letters to the opposite. It also has brightness, color contrast, and zoom features. Some systems have models that work with word processing machines with a CRT.

There is one device that allows a blind person to read any printed material. Using that system, a typist can read an 8-1/2 × 11-in. paper in a few minutes. A small portable case allows the typist to place one hand inside, feeling the images and "reading" with the index finger resting upon a transmitter plate. This device it called The Optican, OPtical, or TActile CONverter. Available very soon will be a portable module, which will convert the output into natural-sounding synthetic speech. An automatic scanning system will have voice output, both hand and automatic versions.

Blind operators can even proofread their own material through the use of a voice synthesizer. Instructions recorded on casettes can teach the blind person how to operate the machine. Braille writing instructions for operating the equipment are also available. Speech can be slowed or sped up. Audio output formats are available in the following: *Pronounce* format, *Punctuate* format, and *Spell* format.

A sophisticated word processing program is Braille-Edit. This allows blind and sighted persons to work together, using microcomputers. A broad range of translation, formatting, and printing operations are included. There are many additional features for blind, sighted, or partially sighted persons.

Two additional helps: Norelco produces a minicassette or "ultra" minicassette marked by a series of ridges in the uper right corner of side one. Photocopy equipment is available that produces raised copy images.

For more information on equipment, you may write:

American Foundation for the Blind
15 West 16th Street
New York, New York 10011

KEY IDEA: COPIES AND PHOTOCOPIERS

Carbon copies are out. Photocopies are in. If you need multiple copies and you are using equipment without that capability, a photocopier is an extremely important piece of equipment. It should be

1. Easy to operate
2. Able to use any type of paper
3. One that produces original-appearing copies
4. One with a low rate of breakdown

SUMMARY

Equipment available is very varied. Exciting advances are being developed almost daily. Physically challenged people have special equipment available to aid them. A person seeking to be his or her own boss has many sources for equipment that will perform well, and on which a good job can be done.

LEARNING ACTIVITIES

ACTIVITY 2-1

1. Name the three types of typewriters available: ________, ____________________, and ____________________.
2. Give two attachments necessary to transcribe from the transcription equipment: ____________________ and ____________________.
3. How can copying machines be helpful to the transcriptionist? ____
4. What is the greatest enemy of all equipment? __________
5. Name three advances that assist the visually impaired in performing transcription: (1) ____________________, (2) ____________________, and (3) ____________________.
6. Give four types of desktop dictation equipment that can be used in transcription: (1) ____________________, (2) ____________________, (3) ____________________, and (4) ____________________.
7. Besides desktop equipment, what else is used for dictating? ____.
8. List some accessory equipment that is needed for transcribing: ____.

ACTIVITY 2-2

Fill in the proper word from the terminology listed at the beginning of this chapter.

1. ____________________ Conversion of recorded dictation to hard copy.
2. ____________________ The roller against which the keys strike.
3. ____________________ That section of the computer where instructions, data, and information are stored to be retrieved at a later date.

4. ______________	A document; written, typed, or printed copy.
5. ______________	The text that appears on the screen *or* a command to produce a specific text on the CRT.
6. ______________	A lighted or blinking indicator on a CRT screen. It indicates the place for entering new text or correcting same.
7. ______________	Magnetic storage device; it can be made of flexible plastic or rigid material.
8. ______________	Any device that produces sound.
9. ______________	The physical components of a computer system.
10. ______________	Display terminal, similar to a television screen, attached to word processing equipment.
11. ______________	A list of previously stored items displayed on a CRT screen from which the typist can choose the word processing document to be edited.
12. ______________	Recorded information that is processed, revised, and printed out (the printout).
13. ______________	To find stored information.
14. ______________	Like typing, except that it includes extra instruction keys of a word-processing machine.
15. ______________	To revise or correct text.
16. ______________	The key used to enter a specified command into word processing equipment.
17. ______________	A given number of bits known as a unit of computer storage.
18. ______________	Ability to move the text horizontally or vertically and to flip document pages on a CRT.

19. ______________________ Acronym for MOdulator DEModulator unit; a device that converts data into signals for telephone transmission, and at the other end, back again into data.

20. ______________________ Software.

NOTES

CHAPTER 3

Grammar

OBJECTIVES

Given instruction and brief written exercises of review, the student will, with 90 to 100 percent accuracy:

1. Recall the eight different parts of speech by definition.
2. Correctly identify given words as the parts of speech in sentences.
3. Demonstrate, in correct grammatical terms, the meaning of transcribing terms and phrases.

KEY IDEA: WHY GRAMMAR IS IMPORTANT

To be a transcriptionist, it is important for you to be proficient in grammar. In your work, you will sometimes need to correct grammatical errors, reword a phrase, or rearrange a sentence in order to send out a document that will properly represent the originator. Your knowledge of correct grammar can be an extremely important asset, while the lack of it can be detrimental. The more easily you can correct a dictation error, the more accurate and impressive your copies will be.

KEY IDEA: PARTS OF SPEECH

This section is not intended as an in-depth study on the parts of speech. It is meant as a simple tool to teach you, or to help you recall that which you already know. A quick summary of the parts of speech is given below, and each is discussed in more detail in the chapter. Review activities will help you test your grasp and recall of the information.

NOUN	Common or proper name of a person, place, or thing	
	Example:	*Susan* prefers *skirts* to *jeans*. (proper) (common)
PRONOUN	Takes the place of a noun	
	Example:	*You* and *she* run fast.
ADJECTIVE	Modifies a noun or pronoun	
	Examples:	That was an *unnerving* ride. They are *noisy*.
VERB	Shows action or state of being to help make a statement	
	Examples:	She *began to work*. The nurse *is* happy.
ADVERB	Modifies a verb, adjective, or another verb.	
	Examples:	Interns learn *quickly*. Are doctors *always* right? He jumps *quite* high.
PREPOSITION	Relates a noun or pronoun to another word	
	Example:	The balls are *in* the yard, *under* the tree, *near* the house.
CONJUNCTION	Joins words, phrases, or clauses	
	Example:	The doctor *and* nurse are a team.
INTERJECTION	Shows or expresses strong emotion	
	Examples:	*Oh*, my goodness! *Ugh*, how horrible!

KEY IDEA: NOUNS

Remember that a noun is the name of a person, place, thing, or class of things. There are common and proper nouns:

Examples: common— lake
proper— Lake Louise

common— city
proper— New York City

KEY IDEA: PRONOUNS USED TO REPLACE NOUNS

A pronoun is a word used in place of a noun; it may be used in place of more than one noun.

Example: Jennie was hired at the Orange Clinic on Monday. *She* liked her job very much. Lori and Susan were hired on Tuesday. *They* were also happy there.

In the example, *she* and *her* are used in place of Jennie. *They* is used in place of Lori and Susan.

Personal Pronouns

The examples above were personal pronouns. They can be used in one of three ways:

First person. The person talking about himself or herself.

Examples: *I, my, mine, me*, or *we, our, ours, us*

Second person. The person being spoken to.

Examples: *You, your, yours*

Third person. The person being spoken about.

Examples: *he, his, him, she, her, hers, it, its, they, theirs, them*

Relative Pronouns

Relative pronouns are used to introduce nouns or noun clauses. They are also used in adjective clauses and use the words *who, whom, whose, which, that.*

Example: The book *that* I borrowed from the library was about the history of medicine.

Other Pronouns

Interrogative Used in questioning: *Who? Whom? What? Whose? Which?*

Example: *Who* was your former doctor?

Demonstrative. Points out a specific person or thing: *This, that, these, those.*

Example: *This* is the book I meant.

Indefinite. Does not refer to a definite person or thing: *somebody, some, all, everyone, few, many, nobody, none.*

Example: *Everyone* wanted to go swimming.

Reflexive. The self form, both singular and plural: *myself, yourself, himself, herself, itself, yourselves,* and *themselves.*

KEY IDEA: ADJECTIVES MODIFY

Adjectives are words used to make the meaning of the noun or pronoun more definitive. They are called *modifiers.* These modifiers may tell *what kind.* See below.

Examples: *white* uniform
old method
weak muscles

Adjectives may also indicate *which one.*

Examples: *this* hospital
those books
that EKG

Or they may tell *how many.*

Examples: *five* doctors
two nurses
several aides

KEY IDEA: ARTICLES ARE ADJECTIVES

The most frequently used adjectives are *a, an,* and *the.* These are usually called *articles* and can be definite or indefinite. *Rule:* Use *a* before words beginning with a consonant or a consonant sound; use *an* before words beginning with a vowel or a vowel sound.

Examples: *A* doctor helped us.
The nurse sat with the patient for *an* hour.
The surgeon was *an* artist.
An x-ray was taken.

KEY IDEA: VERBS EXPRESS ACTION

The verb is a word that expresses action or otherwise helps to make a statement. There are two types of action verbs, but it is necessary only to identify them here as action verbs.

Some action verbs, like *jump, sing, shout,* can be seen or heard, but others cannot. Action verbs that cannot be seen or heard include: *think, evaluate, distrust.*

Examples: (Seen) The doctor *injected* her.
(Unseen). The patient *distrusts* him.

KEY IDEA: VERBS THAT JOIN

Linking verbs help to make a statement by serving as a link between two words. The most common of these are forms of the verb *be*.

Examples: *am, are, is, was, were, be, been, being.*

Any verb phrase ending in *be (can be, will be) or been* (had been, might have been) is a form of the *be* verb.

There are other common linking verbs, such as *appear, become, feel, grow, remain, smell, sound, stay,* and *taste.*

Examples: The patient *feels* well.
The blood level *remains* constant.
The diagnosis *appears* to be correct.
Her condition *stays* the same.
The coffee *tastes* good.

KEY IDEA: ADVERBS ARE MODIFIERS

An adverb is a word used to modify a verb, adjective, or another adverb. It qualifies the meaning of words by answering the questions of *how, when, where,* or *to what extent.*

Many adverbs end in *ly*, but certainly not all of them.

Examples: *always, never, very, soon, not, too*

KEY IDEA: ADVERBS MODIFY ADJECTIVES

Some adverbs modify adjectives.

Examples: Medicine companies have *fiercely* competitive prices. (modifies competitive)
Her patient was *exceptionally* brave. (modifies brave)

KEY IDEA: ADVERBS MODIFY ADVERBS

An adverb may also modify other adverbs.

Example: The patient spoke *too* quickly.

Quickly is the adverb telling *how* the patient spoke. *Too* tells *how* quickly.

KEY IDEA: PREPOSITIONS SHOW RELATIONSHIP

Prepositions are words that combine with a noun or a pronoun to show a relationship to another word in the sentence.

Examples: The doctor rode *past* the hospital.
He parked *near* the hydrant and looked *across* the street.

At, after, by, for, from, in, of, on, since, to, and *until* are easily recognized prepositions.

There are many other commonly used prepositions:

about	*besides*	*outside*
above	*between*	*over*
across	*beyond*	*past*
against	*concerning*	*through*
along	*down*	*toward*
amid	*during*	*under*
among	*except*	*underneath*
around	*inside*	*up*
before	*into*	*upon*
behind	*like*	*with*
below	*near*	*within*
beneath	*off*	*without*
beside	*onto*	

Sometimes prepositions consist of more than one word. They are called compound prepositions. Here is a list of nine:

according to	*in spite of*
because of	*instead of*
by means of	*on account of*
in addition to	*prior to*
in front of	

Depending on its use in a sentence, a word may be either a preposition or an adverb.

Example: The child climbed *down.* (adverb)
or
The child climbed *down* the ladder. (preposition)

KEY IDEA: CONJUNCTIONS JOIN

The conjunction is probably the easiest part of speech to recognize. It joins words or groups of words. The parts joined may be words, phrases, or clauses that function in the same way or in a closely related way.

There are three types of conjunctions: *coordinating, correlating,* and *subordinating.*

Coordinating Conjunctions

Join equal parts of a sentence.

Examples: *and, but, or, nor, for, so, yet*

Correlative Conjunctions

Are used in pairs.

Examples: *either-or, neither-nor, both-and, not only-but also*

Subordinating Conjunctions

Introduce adverb clauses, a subordinate part of the sentence that cannot stand alone. They do not serve a function within the clause they introduce.

Examples: *after, although, as, as if, as long as, as soon as, because, before, if, in order that, since, so that, than, though, unless, until, when, whenever, where, wherever,* and *while*

Many of the above words can be used as other parts of speech. You will recognize some that can be used as prepositions.

KEY IDEA: INTERJECTIONS EXPRESS EMOTION

An interjection expresses emotion. It has no grammatical relation to other words in the sentence.

Sudden or strong feeling, such as anger, fright, excitement, or joy have relatively few words to express them. These words are followed by an exclamation mark.

Examples: *Ouch! Wow! Oops! Oh! No!*

Mild emotion in interjections is followed by a comma.

Example: *Well,* I really don't know.

LEARNING ACTIVITIES

ACTIVITY 3-1

This will be a diagnostic test on the parts of speech. It will reveal where your weaknesses are so you may concentrate on them.

Identify the underlined words as one of the parts of speech. On a separate piece of paper, type the word and the part of speech that it is.

1. In my <u>thirty</u> years of medicine, I have driven <u>over</u> 10,000 miles to attend seminars and workshops.
2. When <u>meetings</u> <u>were</u> over, items bought had to <u>be</u> <u>shipped</u> home.
3. During this <u>period</u>, a map <u>became</u> my constant companion.
4. <u>Magazine</u> articles <u>about</u> health filled <u>my</u> evening hours.

5. I became an ardent learner and continually sought new avenues of learning.
6. My imagination was fired, and I pictured myself as another Madame Curie.
7. The advent of antibiotics brought tremendous improvement in the treatment of infections.
8. Mammograms also provided an early way to detect breast cancer.
9. Miracle-like cures are being accomplished by the use of biofeedback.
10. Oh, how exciting are the experiments and research in medicine today!

How did you do? Take a few minutes to check yourself. Obtain the key from your instructor. Each correct answer is worth four points. Review the definition for any parts of speech you missed.

ACTIVITY 3-2

Pick out the underlined words and type them under the headings of *Proper Nouns* or *Common Nouns*. Check your key. Each correct answer equals five points.

1. Susan Johnson, outspoken leader for women's rights, was born in Akron, Ohio.
2. She was educated in all the humanities and graduated with honors.
3. At an early age, she became interested in medicine.
4. By the time Susan was sixteen, she knew she wanted to become a doctor, a gynecologist.
5. In college, Ms. Johnson took an active role in opposing inequality between the sexes, and soon became known as the young activist for sexual equality in the workplace.
6. Soon after that, Susan was joined by a friend, Esther Sooner, who felt as strongly as she did; they began an organization to promote equal pay for women.

ACTIVITY 3-3

For each common noun below, give a proper noun. Write the answer.

1. hospital ________________________________

2. group ______________________
3. association ______________________
4. clinic ______________________
5. organization ______________________
6. town ______________________
7. office ______________________
8. doctor ______________________
9. nurse ______________________
10 insurance ______________________

ACTIVITY 3-4

For each proper noun given, write in the spaces below a common name you could use.

1. Theater of Performing Arts ______________________
2. Washington Monument ______________________
3. Lake Elsinore ______________________
4. Queen Mary ______________________
5. Los Angeles ______________________
6. Mount Rushmore ______________________
7. John Greenleaf Whittier ______________________
8. Oahu ______________________
9. General Eisenhower ______________________
10. Mayo Clinic ______________________

ACTIVITY 3-5

It is not necessary to identify the *type* of pronoun, but it is important to recognize it as a pronoun. Number 1 to 7 on a separate piece of paper. Pick out the pronoun(s) in each sentence and list it (them) beside the sentence number. Note that the words are *not* underlined, but the number at the end of the sentence indicates how many pronouns are in that sentence.

1. Everyone is interested in medicine, but few people enjoy going to a doctor. (1)
2. Last summer, several friends entered a nursing school that they think is great. (2)

3. At school, many learned to give injections as painlessly as possible. (1)
4. A group of them were eager to learn venipuncture. (1)
5. One of the instructors showed those who were interested how it was done. (4)
6. Each of her instructions was easy to follow, and everyone agreed to learn everything possible. (4)
7. Don't you agree that anything is easier if it is demonstrated first? (3)

ACTIVITY 3-6

In the recognition activity that follows, identify the adjectives by retyping the sentences and underlining the adjectives. There are 37 in all.

1. An extraordinary craze for bicycling swept the United States in the late 1880s.
2. The early versions of the bicycle gave an awkward ride.
3. These ungainly cycles, with a tall wheel in front and a small wheel in back, caused numerous falls.
4. Consequently, many doctors treated injuries caused by bicycle accidents.
5. A more sensible vehicle was introduced in 1885, more like the modern bicycle.
6. Energetic, healthy people became fanatic bicycle riders.
7. Soon bicycling was a national sport.
8. Special clubs for cyclists were organized, and vigorous tours of twenty miles or more became common.
9. Races also became popular with enthusiastic participants and spectators.
10. More accidents happened and emergency treatment flourished.

ACTIVITY 3-7

Identify the action verbs by typing them. There are a total of nine.

1. The nurse administered an injection to the boy.
2. The boy reacted by crying.
3. He also kicked at the nurse.

4. The door opened to let the doctor in.
5. The pediatrician delivered a girl.
6. This pleased the father very much.
7. The surgeon jumped and dropped his scalpel.
8. The O.R. tech handed him a new one.

ACTIVITY 3-8

Type a sentence using each of the *linking verbs* on page 35. There are 23.

ACTIVITY 3-9

Identify the adverbs in the following sentences, and tell which questions they answer: *how, when, where,* or *to what extent.* Type both the word and the question answered.

1. The nurse spoke kindly to the patient.
2. Her patient answered quickly.
3. She then turned away and became exceedingly quiet.
4. Another patient walked toward the therapist.
5. "I'll return tomorrow," she said.
6. She spoke while constantly chewing gum.
7. The therapist was soon exhausted.
8. Another patient arrived late for her appointment.

ACTIVITY 3-10

Tell which adjective is being modified by the underlined adverb. Type your answers and check them.

1. An <u>immensely</u> long surgery began at 6 a.m.
2. Both nurses were needed to move <u>unusually</u> heavy patients.
3. The treatment is <u>fairly</u> hazardous.
4. A <u>moderately</u> hard exercise can be beneficial.
5. When exercise is <u>too</u> vigorous, it can be harmful.
6. Mild exercise offers relief to <u>thoroughly</u> tired bones and muscles.

ACTIVITY 3-11

Tell which adverb is being modified by the underlined word.

1. The diagnosis was concluded quite early and was good news.
2. She reacted very happily to the news.
3. Friends celebrated extremely enthusiastically with her.
4. Test results are sometimes late.
5. Those results were received late yesterday.

ACTIVITY 3-12

Choose ten of the common prepositions that you do not ordinarily use and five of the compound prepositions. Write a sentence using each of them. Underline the preposition.

ACTIVITY 3-13

There is a conjunction underlined in each sentence below. Identify which type it is and write or type your answer. Check and correct.

1. Before the nurse left the office, she turned off the lights.
2. As long as the doctor starts golfing early, he will arrive in time.
3. Miss Jones sounds as if she has caught a cold.
4. Neither the doctor nor the nurse saw the patient leave.
5. Both Dr. Brown and Dr. Smith were on vacation.
6. It was no pleasure trip for either Dr. Brown or Dr. Smith; they were taking more continuing education courses.
7. Dr. Brown returned in three weeks, but Dr. Smith was gone for four weeks.
8. A patient developed complications, so Dr. Brown was called home.
9. Dr. Smith felt deserted, yet he was happy to continue studies.

ACTIVITY 3-14

Type a list of 8 to 10 interjections and show proper punctuation after each one. Your instructor will correct your work.

KEY IDEA: REVIEW AND RECAP

Posttest: Parts of Speech

Read the following sentences and identify the underlined words for the eight parts of speech. Type your answers; there are a total of 24. Check and correct.

1. After five years of general office work, she was working harder than ever for a doctor.
2. It was a new and exciting career, and she loved it.
3. Most of the people who took part in the discoveries of medicine remain nameless.
4. Doctors in training learn quite early to shift for themselves.
5. Itinerant doctors, traveling from place to place, experienced few comforts.
6. When the doctor examines a patient's abdomen, she will often say, "Ouch!"
7. "Oops!" the doctor said, as he dropped his scalpel.

SUMMARY

The goal of every transcriptionist should be to produce a record or report that is accurate in content and grammatically correct. This chapter was designed to help you review the parts of speech and prepare you for your role.

NOTES

CHAPTER 4

Punctuation

OBJECTIVES

After reading this chapter and hearing a lecture on punctuation, the student will, through recall and review, be able to:

1. Perform tests, exercises, and learning activities with a 70 percent accuracy.
2. Punctuate transcribed material with 90 to 100 percent accuracy.

KEY IDEA: PUNCTUATION FOR CLARITY

Punctuation is necessary in all writing in order to make it understandable. Something must let you know when one thought ends and another begins. Voice inflecton and intensity of expression or feeling can be changed or communicated by punctuation. Those discussed here will include sentence endings, commas, colons, semicolons, hyphens, and so on. Each is used for clarity of the written word.

KEY IDEA: FINISH A SENTENCE WITH SOMETHING

Every sentence or statement will have a mark of punctuation at the end. A sentence that *tells* something has a *period*.

Example: The doctor's diagnosis was unexpected.

A sentence that *asks a question* has a *question mark* at the end.

Example: Was your appointment today?

A sentence that *instructs* or *commands* will have a *period.* If the command or instruction is *urgent*, it can end with an *exclamation mark.*

Examples: Nurse, please close the door.
Susan, close that door now!

A sentence that *exclaims* with enthusiasm or emotion also ends with an *exclamation mark.*

Example: What a tremendous idea that is!

KEY IDEA: COMMAS—ENOUGH, BUT NOT TOO MUCH PUNCTUATION

Commas can cause many problems unless you know a few simple rules. Too much punctuation is as confusing as too little. A good rule is "When in doubt, leave it out."

Dates require a comma between the day and the year.

Example: March 29, 19XX

If the year is not followed by a semicolon, period, question mark, or exclamation mark to end the sentence, a comma is placed after the year also.

Examples: On March 29, 19XX, Shari was born.
On July 30, 19XX, she cut her first tooth.
She took her first steps on December 15, 19XX

KEY IDEA: COMMAS AND PLACES

Commas are placed after the following:

1. The name of a town, village, or city.

   Examples: Rochester, New York
   DeQueen, Arkansas

2. Post office box number or rural route number. (There is no comma between state and ZIP code.)

   Examples: Rural Route 3, Nashville, TN
   Box 5103, Garden Grove, CA 92640

3. The name of a county, state, or country.

   Examples: County of Orange, California
   State of California, United States of America
   U.S.A., Continent of North America

4. After the greeting (salutation) of a *personal* leter, and after the closing of any letter.

Examples:

Salutation	*Closing*
Dear Sally,	Sincerely yours,
Dear Dad,	Yours truly,

KEY IDEA: COMMAS IN A SERIES

Use commas to separate a group of *related words* in a series.

Examples: Cynthia, Marian, and Alice have decided to become nurses. They will have a lot of studies in biology, chemistry, anatomy, and physiology.

Commas are also used to separate *related phrases* in a series.

Example: The hospital is an organization governed by a board of directors, the overseeing administrator, and a group of doctor trustees.

Commas are used to separate *subordinate clauses* in a series.

Example: The student doctors will pass their tests if they take good notes, if they study hard, and if they get a good night's sleep.

The last comma is left off if the last two items in a series are joined together.

Example: The nurses' club elected a president, a vice president, and a secretary-treasurer.

The patient's operation consisted of a face lift, a tummy tuck and a liposuction.

Note that items joined by *and*, *or*, or *nor* are not separated by commas.

Independent Clauses

Short independent clauses *may be* separated by commas, but semicolons usually separate independent clauses.

Example: As doctors interested in physical fitness, we jogged, we swam, and we went to the gym.

Compound Sentences

Compound sentences are two independent clauses joined together by coordinating conjuntions, such as : *and, but, or, for*, or *yet*.

Example: They scrubbed down the operating table, *and* then they had a picnic on it.

Nonessential Clauses and Phrases

A nonessential clause is one that is not essential to the sentence but adds extra information or explains something more. These clauses are set off by commas and could be omitted without changing the meaning of the sentence.

Example: Mark Hatfield, an intern, works with Dr. Stone.

Essential clauses, on the other hand, do not need commas. Most of these clauses are introduced by *that.*

Example: The student books that are required are known as texts.

KEY IDEA: COMMAS SEPARATE INTRODUCTORY ELEMENTS

Commas are used after such words as *yes, no, well,* and *why* when they begin a sentence. Exclamations, if not followed by an exclamation mark, are set off by commas: for example, *wow, good grief,* and *gee whiz.*

Examples: Yes, I still have to take the biology exam.
No, I don't want to take the time off.
Well, it could cause trouble.
Good grief, it's time to go!

Use a comma after a participial phrase used as an introduction.

Example: The lights having gone out, we studied by moonlight.

Also use a comma after a succession of introductory prepositional phrases.

Example: In the darkness, by the light of the moon, the situation appeared romantic.

Finally, commas are used after an introductory adverb clause.

Example: After they took a three-and-a-half hour exam, twelve of the students stayed up all night.

KEY IDEA: SEMICOLONS SAY "PAUSE"

The semicolon says to pause just a little longer than you do for a comma, but a shorter pause than is necessary for a period.

There are four reasons to use a semicolon. They are:

1. Between independent clauses if they are not joined by the conjunctions *and, but, or, nor, for, so,* or *yet.* This is especially true if the clauses are very closely connected.

   Example: Ima Love was elected president of the Nurses' Association; she truly deserved the recognition.

2. Between independent clauses, when joined by this long list of words: *for example, for instance, that is, accordingly, besides, moreover, nevertheless, however, furthermore, consequently, instead, otherwise, therefore,* and *hence.*

   Example: Only two people came for the CPR class; consequently, the class was canceled.

3. To separate independent clauses joined by a coordinating conjunction, if there are commas in the clause.

   Example: The disease of Chlamydia, left untreated in men, may cause sterility; but, in women, it can lead to P.I.D.

4. Between items in a series that already contain commas.

   Example: There are famous hospitals in all of these cities: Los Angeles, California; Dallas, Texas; Rochester, New York; and Chicago, Illinois.

KEY IDEA: COLONS AND FOLLOWERS

Whether the text says it or not, a colon means "notice what is following." It is used as below.

1. To note what follows.

   Example: The nursing students were allowed four pieces of equipment in their exam area: stethoscopes, blood pressure cuffs (sphygmomanometers), thermometers, and wristwatches.

2. Before a long, formal statement or quotation.

   Example: Psychologists tell us: "The bad taste of cold coffee may be more in your head than in your mug."

2. In certain conventional situations.
   a. Between the hour and the minutes in writing time.

   Examples: 8:20 a.m.
   9:50 tonight

   b. Between chapter and verse in Bible passages.

Examples: Matthew 6:33
John 3:16

c. After the salutation (greeting) of a business letter.

Examples: Dear Dr. Stitchem:
Gentlemen:

KEY IDEA: UNDERLINE TO ITALICIZE

Underlining is used when you want something in italics. It is used in the following instances:

1. Titles of books, periodicals, works of art, films, TV programs, statues, planes, trains, and so on.

Examples: *The Call of the Wild* (book)
the *Venus de Milo* (statue)
The Journal of the American Medical Association (magazine)
the *Queen Mary* (ship)

2. Words, letters, and figures referred to as such, and foreign words not yet in the English language.

Examples: What does the *A* stand for?
Try writing compound sentences without using *and*.
There are a lot of *1's* in my phone number.
The genus *Vulpes* includes the red fox.

KEY IDEA: QUOTATION MARKS SHOW EXACT WORDS

Whenever you use quotation marks, it is usually to show that someone's exact words are being used. Quotation marks are always in pairs, one at the beginning of the quote and one at the end.

Note that the direct quote *begins* with a capital letter.

Examples: "Walking down the hill is harder than going up," Shari remarked.
The nurse asked, "When do we get our uniforms?"

When a quotation is divided by an interrupting expression, you use two sets of quotation marks; the second part of the quote is not capitalized.

Example: "Remember," said the doctor, "you must be at the hospital at 6 a.m."

The direct quote is set off from the rest of the sentence by a comma, question mark, or exclamation point.

Examples: "Where are we going?" asked Ann.

"We're going to the doctor's office first," Helen replied.

"I don't want to go there!" exclaimed Ann.

Other uses of quotation marks are enumerated below:

1. *Commas, periods, question marks,* and *exclamation marks* are most often placed inside the quotation marks. See the previous examples. Exception: meaning can change this.

   Example: Did John say, "I'm not going"?

2. *Colons* and *semicolons* are always placed outside the quotation marks.

   Examples: The doctor said jokingly, "A stitch in time saves nine"; however, it sounded strange coming from a surgeon.

   The following medications were considered "miracle drugs": sulfa, insulin, and penicillin.

3. Writing dialogue occurs infrequently, if ever, in medical transcription. If it does, you begin a new paragraph with each speaker.
4. When a quoted passage consists of more than one quoted paragraph, begin each paragraph with quotes and use another one at the end of the entire passage.
5. Titles of short stories, poems, songs, chapters, articles, and parts of books and periodicals are enclosed in quotation marks. This is probably not pertinent to any medical transcription unless you are typing manuscripts. The length of the written work would determine whether it would be in quotation marks or italics.
6. Enclose slang words, technical terms, and other expressions that are unusual in English in quotation marks or underscore.

   Example: Interns sometimes "hang out" at a local restaurant.

KEY IDEA: APOSTROPHES INDICATE RELATIONSHIP

The apostrophe is used with a noun or a pronoun to indicate ownership or relationship.

In English, you indicate the possessive case by adding an apostrophe *s*, or sometimes, merely an apostrophe, to the noun. Plural words ending in *s* usually require only an apostrophe.

Examples: the nurse's uniform (one nurse)

the nurses' schedule (more than one nurse)

the bus's open door

The most common use of apostrophes is in contractions, where letters have been omitted.

Example: I have— I've
you are— you're
it is— it's
is not— isn't
do not— don't
have not— haven't

KEY IDEA: HYPHENS DIVIDE AND JOIN

Hyphens are used for two reasons. The first reason is to divide words at the end of a line. Always divide between syllables. If you have a question where to divide, consult the dictionary.

Examples: doc-tor
ortho-pedist

Words containing double consonants are usually divided between the consonants.

Examples: tonsil-lectomy
ap-pendectomy
but bill-ing, *not* bil-ling

Words with a prefix or suffix should be divided between the prefix and root or the root and suffix.

Examples: pre-scription
spoon-ful

Already hyphenated words should be divided only where the hyphen already exists.

Examples: self-destructive
happy-go-lucky

The second reason hyphens are used is to join the parts of compound words; however, the tendency is toward making two words instead of the one-word compound.

Examples: present-day policy
up-to-date techniques

Compound numbers are also joined with hyphens.

Examples: thirty-three
three-and-one-half

Use a hyphen in words with the prefixes *all-*, *ex-*, *self-*, and with the suffix *-elect*.

Examples: self-contained
ex-secretary
all-American
President-elect

Finally, when an adjective precedes the noun it modifies, it is hyphenated.

Examples: middle-class neighborhood
first-time swimmer

KEY IDEA: DASHES INDICATE A BREAK

Dashes indicate an abrupt break in thought. In typing, you strike the hyphen key twice to indicate a dash and do not leave a space before or after the two hyphens.

Examples: The surgery for tomorrow--I forgot to tell you--has been cancelled.

When Jerry was born--he was the last of the quadruplets--we weren't sure he would make it.

A dash is also used to mean *namely, that is, in other words* (or the like) before an explanation.

Examples: This is the best hospital food in town--they have a wonderful salad bar.

They need three full schedules in a hospital--7–3, 3–11, and 11–7.

KEY IDEA: PARENTHESES INCLUDE MINOR MATERIAL

Material added to a sentence, but not considered of major importance, is enclosed in parentheses. Punctuation marks that belong to the parenthetical material are placed within the parentheses. They are placed outside the parentheses when the belong to the sentence as a whole.

Examples: The patient was given numerous tests (Were they all necessary?) before being told there was nothing wrong.

The nurse tried on numerous uniforms ("Gee! they are all so expensive!") before deciding on one.

LEARNING ACTIVITIES

ACTIVITY 4-1

Read through the following paragraph; then retype it, punctuating it correctly.

What is the surgery schedule like at White Memorial today Well today it begins at 630 a m Dr Brown begins with a tonsillectomy at that time Dr Jones follows with a hysterectomy Dr D Liver then has a C Section After that Dr Cutem is doing a gallbladder That brings us up to noon Oh my goodness we also have an emergency appendectomy No one will have lunch today.

Check your answers with the key, which you may obtain from your instructor.

ACTIVITY 4-2

Retype the sentences below, placing commas wherever needed. Check and correct your work.

1. Jill went to San Francisco California on March 2 1990.
2. Sharon Susan and Anthony plan to go to New York for a vacation.
3. They plan among other things to study nutrition and health.
4. For many people in the world vegetables are their only staple food.
5. Whole grains such as rice barley corn oats and rice feed millions.
6. For over 5000 years the soybean which is high in protein has been used abundantly by most oriental people.
7. Consequently they soon learned that meat is not absolutely necessary regardless of how it's promoted.
8. As beautiful wholesome and healthy women they didn't appear to need nutritional studies.
9. Anthony on the other hand was pale anemic and sickly-looking.
10. Yes he appeared to need everything. In fact he said "Ladies this can be a great benefit to me. I love it!"

ACTIVITY 4-3

Retype the information below, putting in colons and semicolons where needed. Correct your work when finished. (There are a total of ten.)

1. Many people won't use bread however, it is a good source of protein, riboflavin, iron, and thiamine.

2. The overcast sky threatened rain however, the hike was continued.
3. Esther won the Miss Health Contest she certainly looked both healthy and beautiful.
4. Contestants came from all these cities Paris, France London, England New York, New York Pittsburg, Pennsylvania and many others.
5. Nutrition enthusiasts tell us "Beauty and health begin nine months before birth while the child is still in the mother's womb."
6. Precisely at 900 a.m. the student stood and read Psalm 91 1–6.

ACTIVITY 4-4

Retype these sentences and underline where needed. Correct your work, using the key.

1. The Nightingales was a popular, rather risque TV program.
2. Many people consider 13 as bad luck.
3. The Orange County Association of Medical Assistants took a trip to see the Spruce Goose and the Queen Mary.
4. The Physician's Management has been a wonderful help to office managers.
5. One of the longest-running "soaps" was General Hospital.

ACTIVITY 4-5

Retype the following information, using underlining and quotation marks where needed. If necessary, set it up differently from what it is.

1. What are you doing with that tiger? asked Leon. You should take him to the zoo. I did take him to the zoo, Harry replied. Leon asked, Then what is he doing here? He enjoyed it so much that now we're going to a movie! exclaimed Harry.
2. Being in a hurry, the doctor said, Give me a ham on rye, and make it quick.
3. Another customer asked, When do you have to return?
4. As soon as possible, replied the doctor.
5. I don't have a watch, said the doctor. What time is it now?

6. The conversation turned to interns known as jocks: Tom, Dick, and Harry.
7. Mark Twain's writing ability was well demonstrated in Tom Sawyer.
8. His humor shone in the story, The Celebrated Jumping Frog of Calvaras County.
9. Fog, by Carl Sandburg, was very explicit.
10. Who was the author of Hawaii and The Source?
11. I always wondered what the A meant in Jack A. Jackson's name.
12. Gray's Anatomy is a standard textbook for doctors.

ACTIVITY 4-6

Retype the paragraphs below, inserting hyphens and dashes where appropriate.

1. Roughly one quarter of Americans have high blood cholesterol levels putting them at risk for heart disease.
2. After this three and a half hour exam, twelve of the students stayed up all night. (Others got their usual sleep.) Next day, the well rested students improved their scores. The red eyed students scored worse overall than the day before often because they repeatedly tried unsuccessful approaches. If you must pull an "all nighter," better do it before a simple test.

ACTIVITY 4-7

Put in the apostrophes or parentheses where needed when you retype the following sentences.

1. She bought two cents worth of candy.
2. A babys cry can be a startling thing.
3. Womens shoe sizes vary greatly even from one foot to another.
4. Theyve made the knives blades extremely sharp; we wont ever need them sharpened.
5. Anne Murray I have every album is famous world-wide.
6. Show the possessive form for the words below:

scalpel
administrator
nurse
doctor
patient
assistant
typist
transcriptionist

ACTIVITY 4-8

Retype the following sentences, placing hyphens where appropriate.

1. The patient seemed very self sufficient.
2. The pain pill cost $1.42.

ACTIVITY 4-9

Show where to divide these words at the end of a typed line:

allergist
perspiration
grateful
secretary-treasurer
preeminent
excessive
son-in-law

NOTES

CHAPTER 5

Capitalization

OBJECTIVES

Following the reading and studying of this chapter, the student should:

1. Perform all tests, exercises, and learning activities with a 70 percent accuracy. (This excludes pretests.)
2. Demonstrate knowledge and skill when capitalizing original material. See learning activities.

KEY IDEA: DO IT RIGHT

There are a few basic rules for capitalization. Capitalizing a word serves notice of the importance of that word; you also serve notice that your are referring to a *particular* person, place, or thing.

By learning and understanding the rules, by applying them correctly, and by taking pride in your work, you can avoid capitalization errors.

A poorly capitalized document is embarrassing to the sender and poorly received by the recipient.

The basic rules for capitalization follow:

1. Capitalize the first word in every sentence, regardless of the kind of sentence it is.

Example: There is a problem with medication on Four West.

2. Usually the first word in every line of poetry is capitalized.

Example: Flowers bloom in the springtime,
Leaf colors change in the fall
Snow in winter, sun in summer,
And God reigns over all. —NLM

3. The pronoun "I" and the interjection "O" are capitalized.

Example: The line I read was, "Hear us, O Lord."

4. Capitalize proper nouns and proper adjectives:
   a. Names of persons and titles:

Examples: Richard Alton, Jr.
Mark Brown, M.D.
Susan White, D.D.S.

   b. The name of a particular *person, place*, or *thing*. is a proper noun.

Examples:

Common Noun	*Proper Noun*
city	Los Angeles
doctor	Samuel White, M.D.
hospital	White Memorial
rest home	Guardian Rest Home

   c. When a proper noun is used as an adjective, it is a proper adjective. Note that the word modified is *not* capitalized.

Example:

Noun	*Adjective*
France	French horn
Italy	Italian pastry
Ireland	Irish eyes
Mayo	Mayo tray
Lister	Lister bandage scissors

5. Capitalize geographical names—cities, towns, counties, townships, states, countries, continents, islands, bodies of water, mountains, streets and parks, and sections of the country.
6. Capitalize the names of organizations and business firms.

Examples: *Organizations* American Medical Association, California Association of Health Career Educators, American Association of Medical Assistants.

Businesses International Business Machines, American Broadcasting Company, Transworld Airlines.

Institutions and Buildings Empire State Building, University of California at Irvine, Hyatt Hotel.

7. Capitalize the names of government bodies and institutions.

   Examples: The House of Congress, Environmental Protection Agency, Federal Drug Administration.

8. The names of historical and special events and periods should be capitalized.

   Examples: *Historical Events and Periods* World War II, the Yalta Conference, the French Revolution.

   Special Events and Calender Items the Cotton Bowl, Inaugural Adress, Alumni Day, Homecoming Dance, April, Easter, Tuesday, Good Friday.

The same rules (number 5–8 above) apply for abbreviations as well as for the full name. *When in doubt, always consult your dictionary.*

LEARNING ACTIVITIES

ACTIVITY 5-1

Retype and capitalize where needed. Obtain the key and correct, circling any errors you may have missed.

according to lynn robins, a linguist-anthropologist at the university of michigan, we-speech in the doctor's office causes confusion— and sometimes damage.

if a doctor asks, "how are we doing?" do you look to see who else is in the room? robins, in analyzing videotaped interviews, found that doctors use "we" three times more often than patients. when a patient uses the term, he almost always has another family member in mind. for physicians, "we" was used flexibly to mean "i," "you and i," or "all doctors." robin's findings were reported in the magazine *hippocrates*.

ACTIVITY 5-2

Retype the following paragraph, letters, and memo, making all the necessary capitalizations. Check your work with the answer key, marking any errors with an "X" over the mistake.

ACTIVITY 5-2a

on a recent trip, in july, sally visited the southwest. she saw many indians: the hopi, puma, apache, and others. she saw the indian women weaving blankets and the indian men making pottery. some hopi indians were costumed and doing a rain dance. apache warriors were dressed in feathers and painted faces for a mock battle. it was hot and dusty there in sante fe, new mexico. later sally went to albequerque and southwest from there to clovis.

ACTIVITY 5-2b

rames zimbautra
yuffa of nazareth
israel

american historical society
22246 ageless street
anytown, ca 92600

gentlemen:

i soon hope to become a resident of your country; also, a potential citizen. there are many things which i wonder about and seek more information on: the yalta conference and your president franklin d. roosevelt's role in that, world war II and why the united states became involved, thanksgiving day, independence day, the empire state building, the super bowl, the city of los angeles, and the rams. if you can't furnish this information, please tell me where i can get it.

respectfully yours,

rames zimbautra

ACTIVITY 5-2c

to: mcleod surgical supply order dept.
from: dr. xtra's office

we received our order made on may 2, this year. sorry to report the following: mayo stand and tray are scratched, the lister bandage scissors are dull, the rochester-oshner hemostats are missing, and the ace bandages are short. otherwise, the order is fine. please follow up soon.

ACTIVITY 5-2d

261 susan avenue
esther, md 62310
may 1, 19XX

dear fernando,

i hear you have joined the world health organization and that you are going to various islands for work. is it true that you will be in the west indies, the philippines, and the hebrides?

please answer soon. i'm very curious.

your friend,

carlos

ACTIVITY 5-3

Research and type a one- to two-page report on George Washington Carver and his role in science and medicine, if any. Capitalize properly throughout.

NOTES

CHAPTER 6

Numbers

OBJECTIVES

After reading and reviewing this chapter, the student should:

1. Demonstrate by written test an understanding of the numerical terminology, correctly defining ten numerical terms.
2. Demonstrate, through repeated Learning Activities, correct usage of numbers to 100 percent correctness in all different situations.

KEY IDEA: INTRODUCTION TO NUMBERS

In typing numbers, it is sometimes difficult to know when to use the figure and when to spell it out. You may have learned to spell out one to ten, and use figures above ten. This is true as a general rule; however, there are numerous instances where it does not apply. Most of those instances that apply to medical transcription are included here.

The simple term *number* is not as simple as it sounds. The dictionary has more than 20 definitions for this one word. For the sake of clarity, we have selected the one that seems to be most appropriate. The terms and definitions listed here will be reviewed in a Learning Activity later.

KEY TERMS: NUMBER TERMINOLOGY

1. **Number** an element of any of many mathematical systems.
2. **Numeral** a conventional symbol representing a number.
3. **Arabic** of, or relating to, or characteristic of Arabia or the Arabs.
4. **Arabic numeral** figures and combinations of figures 0–9.
5. **Roman** of, or relating to Rome or the people of Rome.
6. **Roman numeral** a numeral in the system based on the Roman system (using letters of the alphabet) in capitals or lowercase.
7. **Numeric term** Any word pertaining to a number or numbering system.
8. **Cardinal number** used in simple counting, or in answer to "how many?" Example: He counted to twelve.
9. **Ordinal number** used to indicate the order or succession of items in the same class (1st, 4th, twelfth).
10. **Figure** a number symbol.

KEY IDEA: MEDICAL REPORTS

In a *medical report*, be consistent with *series or lists*. When the dictator numbers some but not all items in a series, either number them all or not at all. Use Arabic numerals, and number either horizontally or vertically.

Remember also to *capitalize the first letter of each numbered item.*

Examples: The following reports were done:

1. Urinalysis
2. Blood Uric Acid
3. Cholesterol

The following reports were done: (1) Urinalysis, (2) Blood Uric Acid, (3) Cholesterol.

KEY IDEA: NUMBERING PAGES

Usually you number the first page with number 1 at the center of the bottom. Second and third pages should be typed in the upper right-hand corner. Exceptions occur with some word processing or computer programs, which automatically paginate in a different manner.

KEY IDEA: ABBREVIATOINS, NUMBERS, AND SYMBOLS

For *symbols or abbreviations*, use Arabic numerals, leaving a space between the numeral and the abbreviation. *Note:* While the formal rule is to use periods with abbreviations, the current trend is to leave off the "s" on lb and the periods for both weights and measurements (ft, yd, oz, mm). They will be left off here. However, to avoid confusion with the preposition, in. for inches is used.

Examples: Take the medication 1 t.i.d.
The baby weighed 8 lb 1 oz.
Normal urine pH 5.0.
There are 12 in. in a foot.

A *number and a symbol* do not have a space between.

Examples: She had $100 in her purse.
A 10% discount was given.
A #10 Bardic was used.

One exception: when typing numbers with *multiple symbols*, or when *giving measurements*, leave a space between the two. Examples of each of these are given below:

Examples: The tray was 15 × 1 × 24 and had numerous 4 × 4 sponges.
The woman was a very tall 6 ft 1 in.

When writing *plus* or *minus* with a number, use figures and symbols. *Note:* Some equipment might not have symbols as keys; words would be the only method to convey the meaning.

Examples: Albumin 1+
Basal Metabolic Rate ± 5
Muscle reaction –3

Use figures with *metric abbreviations.*

Examples: 2 cc, 10 kg, 4 ml, 5 mm, 6 L

When *two or more symbols* are used together— for example when recording temperatures— either spell them out in full or use the abbreviated form.

Examples: In severe illness temperature may reach 40°C.
In severe illness temperature may reach 40 degrees Celsius.

Electrocardiograms are reported in the combination of Arabic and Roman numerals and abbreviations for the different leads. Written in the order in which they are done, the limb leads are I, II, III, AVR, AVL, AVF. The chest leads are written V^1, V^2, V^3, V^4, V^5, V^6 (or V- 1, V-2, etc.).

KEY IDEA: AGE AND DAY OF MONTH AND YEAR

Use numerals when giving an *age*, unless it is expressed as an indefinite age.

Examples: The baby is only 30 days old.
The mother was in her thirties.

Use figures for the *day of the month and the year*; spell out the month. There are two ways to do this: first, the conventional, and second, the military.

Examples: March 29, 19XX
29 March 19XX

For expressing the *date after the month*, use cardinal numbers (1, 2, 3).

Examples: March 29
Her birthday was October 3.

Use ordinal numbers to express the date *before the month* (1st, 2nd, 3rd, 4th, or 2d, 3d). These are used *only* before the name of the month in combination with the word *of*.

Examples: She was born on the 29th of March.
His appointment was on the 3rd of October.

KEY IDEA: ADDRESSES

For all *addresses* use only one through ten spelled out in full for the *street numbers*. For house or post office box numbers, spell out only "one." For other numbers use numerals. This also applies to route numbers.

Examples: One Old Town Road
2062 Eighth Street
P. O. Box One
Route 2
1601 East 15th Street
P. O. Box 5103
1022 Steele Drive

KEY IDEA: DECIMAL FRACTIONS AND NUMBERS

Some lab tests, medications, and body temperatures are written in *decimal numerals*. Always place a zero before a decimal that is not a whole number. Be consistent by adding a zero after a whole number in a set of decimal fraction numbers.

Examples: Her temperature was 35.2 C (35.2°C).
The specific gravity was 1.012.
The patient was given 0.5 cc. Tetanus Toxoid.

He had two lacerations on the face. One was 3.2 cm and the second was 7.8 cm for a total of 11.0 cm.

The table was 18.0 × 25.4 × 0.5.

Use numerals pertaining to drugs, directions, dosage and strength.

Examples: The prescription was written for Voltaren Tablets 75 mg.

Directions for taking it were Tab 1 q a.m. and p.m. PRN arthritis pain.

Penicillin is usually 300,000 U/cc. A small person would probably receive 600,000 U or 2 cc.

Armour's Thyroid was to be taken 0.5 grain daily with a gradual increase to 2.0 grains.

Use decimals with symbols, or whole numbers as needed with symbols, to express amounts of money.

Examples: Her salary was $2,000 a month.

The hospital stay was $180 a day.

The initial hospital visit was $127.50, and a consultation visit cost her $150.

Less than dollar amounts are written with symbols or spelled out.

Examples: The sum of two coins is 55¢, and one is not a nickel.

She was given 14¢ in change.

She was given 14 cents change.

KEY IDEA: ROMAN NUMERALS

Use Roman numerals, uppercase (I, II) after a person's name. You may also use ordinals, according to the individual's preference.

Examples: James A. Simpson IV

or

James A. Simpson 4th

Use Roman numerals in reporting EKG and EEG leads; also to describe the twelve cranial nerves.

Examples: Limb lead II is considered to be diagnostic.

Cranial lead III shows some abnormality.

Does Bell's Palsy involve cranial nerve VII?

As a general rule, some specialties use Roman numerals, for example, obstetrics and gynecology.

Examples: Gravida III, Para I, Abortion I

Some professionals, however, prefer Arabic numerals in the above examples. In that case, it would be written:

Gravida 3, Para 1, Abortion 1

Other traditional uses in medicine include types, techniques, factors, phases, class, stage, and some test reports, for example, Pap Class II.

KEY IDEA: PLURALS

Numbers are followed by an "s" to form a plural. You do not need an apostrophe, for example, 3s, 4s, 10s. You may write them out if you prefer, but it is not needed.

Examples: threes, fours, tens.

KEY IDEA: NEEDLE AND SUTURE NUMBERS

The larger the number, the smaller the needle or suture. Arabic numerals are used to describe the sizes of suture material; also for needles used for injections and venipuncture. They may also be used to indicate the number of sutures made, although that would ordinarily be written out. Sutures may be written in three ways.

Examples: Many 22G - 1½-in. needles are used for I.M. injections. (22 gauge)

Order 100 #25G - ½-in. needles. (25 gauge)

The plastic surgeon used many fine #7-0 sutures. (pronounced 7 aught)

The plastic surgeon used many fine 7-0 sutures. (7 aught)

The plastic surgeon used many fine #0000000 sutures. (still 7 aught)

2-0 Chromic catgut may be used for deep tissues. (2 aught)

#00 Chromic catgut may be used for deep tissues. (2 aught)

#2-0 Chromic catgut may be used for deep tissues. (2 aught)

10 #5-0 silk sutures were used to close. (5 aught)

Ten #5-0 silk sutures were used to close. (5 aught)

The surgeon used 70 #4-0 nylon sutures. (4 aught)

The surgeon used seventy 4-0 nylon sutures. (4 aught)

KEY IDEA: SUMMARY

Many ways to correctly use numbers have been included here. An attempt was made to cover the majority of situations involving medical transcription. Other questionable situations when encountered could probably be settled by referring to *Medical Transcription Do's and Don'ts* by Fordney and Diehl.

LEARNING ACTIVITIES

ACTIVITY 6-1

Write or type the ten words given, then place the correct number from the matching definition in front of it. Example: 2 error.

___ figure

___ Roman

___ Arabic

___ numeral

___ cardinal number

___ number

___ Roman numeral

___ ordinal number

___ Arabic numeral

___ numeric term

1. An element of any of many mathematical systems.
2. A conventional symbol representing a number.
3. Of, or relating to, or characteristic of Arabia or the Arabs.
4. Figures and combinations of figures 0–9.
5. Of, or relating to Rome or the people of Rome.
6. A numeral in a system based on the Roman system (using letters of the alphabet in capitals or lowercase).
7. Any word pertaining to a number or numbering system.
8. Used in simple counting, or in answer to "how many?" Example: He counted to twelve.
9. Used to indicate the order, or succession, of items in the same class (1st, 4th, twelfth).
10. A number symbol.

ACTIVITY 6-2

Compose two original sentences from each of the Key Idea sections to illustrate the proper use of numbers.

NOTES

CHAPTER 7

Sentence Structure

OBJECTIVES

Following the reading of this chapter, through learning activities, the student will:

1. Recognize both the simple subject and complete subject in sentences.
2. Recognize both the simple predicate and complete predicate.
3. Recognize complement wording.
4. Recognize and construct both simple and complex sentences.
5. Compose brief, understandable, to-the-point sentences.

Everyone composes sentences. Some are written; most are oral. How many times does a person think:

> "I'm composing a sentence. It must have a subject and a predicate. It must not be in fragments but must contain a complete thought."

Very early we learn to make complete sentences, never analyzing them, except in a grammar class. Transcriptionists will often have the job of rearranging sentence structure. For that reason, let us briefly review how it is done.

Every sentence is a group of words, containing a *subject* and *predicate* and conveying a complete thought.

KEY IDEA: SUBJECT

A sentence must refer to someone or something. This is the *subject.*

Example: *Jane bowls.* (simple subject)

A subject may be simple or complete. *Jane* is the simple subject. Any added words that describe, identify, or explain more about Jane would be included in the *complete subject.*

Example: *Jane, the director of Medical Records,* bowls. (complete subject)

KEY IDEA: PREDICATE

A sentence must tell something about that person or thing. The word, or words, that do this are called the *predicate* and always contain a verb.

Example: Jane *bowls.* (simple predicate)

The word *bowls* tells us what Jane does. *Bowls* is the *simple predicate.* Other words that describe *bowls* would be the *complete predicate.* It could tell how, when, or where.

Example: Jane *bowls often at the City Bowl.* (complete predicate— tells when and where)

KEY IDEA: COMPLEMENT

A *complement* is a word or group of words that complete the meaning begun by the subject and predicate.

Example: Jane bowls *well.* (complement)

Well is the word which tells how Jane bowls. It is the complement that completes the thought.

KEY IDEA: COMPLETE THOUGHT, NOT FRAGMENTED

When speaking, we often tend to talk in incomplete sentences. These are called *fragmented sentences.* They are usually understood and accepted orally.

Examples: "Hi, Jane. Where have you been?"
"Doctor's office."
"What's wrong?"
"Trouble with the thyroid."
"Too bad. What are they doing?"
"Running tests. Sure be glad when they're through."

In writing we must not do that. Since we cannot be seen or heard, the written words must convey the whole message. On paper we must express ourselves in complete sentences. Here is a fragmented sentence:

Example: The blanket covered.

Even with a subject and predicate, the above sentence is not a complete thought. There must be more.

Example: The blanket covered the patient.

Now we have a complete sentence.

KEY IDEA: TYPES OF SENTENCES

There are four types of sentences. A *declarative* sentence makes a statement. Most sentences we use are declarative.

Example: The surgery was a long and involved one.

An *imperative* sentence is one that gives a command or makes a request.

Examples: Close that door! (command)
Please pass the butter. (request)

An *interrogative* sentence is one that asks a question.

Example: Will Dr. Zee be able to assist in surgery?

An *exclamatory* sentence is one that expresses strong feeling.

Examples: You should have brought the oxygen immediately!
I really *hate* hot weather!

Simple

Sentences may be structured in several ways. Some expressions are made in *simple sentences.* These are easy and basic to all others.

Example: The patient was sent for a chest x-ray.

Compound

A *compound sentence* makes two separate statements that are closely related.

Example: The patient was sent for a chest x-ray; she also had to get a CBC.

Complex

A *complex sentence* can be long and involved. It can also be compound–complex, and can sometimes be divided into two or more sentences.

Example: The patient is going very early to have a chest x-ray; she is also ordered to get a CBC at the same time, and while she is there, she might as well make an appointment for an upper GI series.

This could easily be broken down into two or three sentences.

KEY IDEA: TRANSCRIPTIONIST'S ROLE

What is the transcriptionist's role in all this? You are the one responsible to make all that you hear presentable and understandable. Sometimes it means that you have to rearrange or restructure sentences *without changing their meaning.*

In recent years, there are more doctors with different language origina doing dictation. Some languages have a different sentence structure from that of English. For this reason, you need to sharpen your listening skills so that you can rearrange the wording into acceptable English. (Different sounds in foreign speech are covered in the proofreading chapter.)

You must never alter facts, but you may rearrange words for proper sentence structure. When dictating, some people ramble, making long and cumbersome sentences. You may be able to make two sentences out of the long and involved ones. Be careful not to lose any of the original meaning.

LEARNING ACTIVITIES

ACTIVITY 7-1

Retype the exercise below. First, find the simple subject and the simple predicate. Draw one line under the simple subject. Draw two lines under the simple predicate. *Note:* Sometimes the subject can come after the predicate.

1. The discovery of radium has been credited to Marie and Pierre Curie.
2. As a student, Marie first discovered the rays of uranium.
3. She called them radioactivity.
4. Marie was born in Poland in 1867.
5. Pierre Curie, a Frenchman, was born in 1859.
6. Soon after their marriage, they began working together.
7. Both radium and polonium were discovered by this pair.

8. In recognition of their discovery, they were awarded the Nobel Prize.

ACTIVITY 7-2

Return to the activity you just finished. Now, draw one line under the complete subject. Draw two lines under the complete predicate.

ACTIVITY 7-3

Rearrange these complex sentences or separate them, making two or more statements. A suggested key is enclosed. Yours does not need to be exactly the same. Just be certain that you haven't altered the facts. If you have any questions about your work, have your teacher check it.

1. This is a well-developed, very well-nourished, white 10-year-old girl who does not appear to be very happy; however, she is very cooperative during the examination.
2. As you may recall, this patient had noted blurred vision for the past several days, prior to being seen in our office, which had improved somewhat during the most recent day or two.
3. His cranial nerves were intact, the discs were flat, the pupils were reactive, visual fields were full, there was no optic atrophy; there were no sensory or cerebellar findings, although he tended to walk on a broad base and to lean to the right.
4. Pneumoencephalograms were not entirely satisfactory, although here again there was some discrepancy between the interpretation by the neurologist and by the roentgenologist.
5. Here, in the clinic today, these two lesions on the right external ear have been anesthetized with 1% Xylocaine and with point desiccation, they have been destroyed and then curetted and dried out with the electrodesiccating current.
6. She was given calcium gluconate, intravenously, which seemed to result in some improvement in uterine tone, which before that was nil; in fact, the uterus was so soft before packing that it could not be palpated.
7. The surface of the brain (we saw the anterior portion of the temporal lobe and the posterior of the frontal lobe)

appeared normal except at approximately the anterior portion on the right middle temporal gyrus.

8. The small piece of bone that had been elevated with the temporal muscle was removed and not replaced while Gelfoam was placed over the brain surface as a substitute for the dura, and the temporal muscle was sutured using 2-0 silk.
9. The nasopharynx was inspected with a mirror, and a rather large and reasonably obstructed adenoid mass was noted and removed in multiple fragments using adenoid curets.

NOTES

CHAPTER 8

Proofreading

OBJECTIVES

After reading the chapter the student will:

1. Recognize and use common proofreading symbols in the learning activities.
2. Explain the importance of proofreading and realize that one error is too many.
3. Type, read, and correct assignments with 100 percent accuracy.
4. Demonstrate through oral practice knowledge of some foreign speech sounds that are different from English.

KEY IDEA: DEFINITION

To proofread is to reread carefully and correct any accuracies in form or mechanics.

KEY IDEA: DOCUMENTS REPRESENT

Why proofread? And why is it so important? Is it not enough to type or print what you hear? Keep in mind that every document represents its sender, and that document conveys to its receiver a picture of its sender. Therefore, the object of every document must be that it should:

1. Be mailable.
2. Be correct in form and appearance.
3. Make the sender appear to be neat, efficient, understandable, and caring.

If there are errors in form or mechanics (spelling, capitalization, and punctuation), it appears that the sender is careless and inefficient. While this may not be true, a negative impression has, nevertheless, been created. As a transcriptionist, you are the one who controls that picture. Proofreading plays a tremendous part in ensuring a perfect document every time, for even one error in a document can be very embarrassing.

Proofreading someone else's material is fairly easy. It is much harder to proofread your own and spot your own errors. For this reason you should read a document before it leaves your typewriter. It is corrected so much more easily while still aligned. Reinserting the paper to correct a mistake is much more difficult. On a word processor, the material can be proofread while still on the screen.

If you are transcribing from an original document, compare the two while your copy is in the machine or on the screen. Most medical documents originate through dictation; they do not have a hard copy for comparison. Therefore, you must learn to depend on your knowledge and discernment. One way, preferred by some, is to quickly make a rough draft, correct it, and retype. Proofread the final copy.

Follow these steps when proofreading:

1. Free yourself of all distractions.
2. Concentrate.
3. Read through two times.
   a. First: for form, appearance, and content. Ask the questions: "Is it clear?" and "Does it make sense?"
   b. Second: for spelling, punctuation, capitalization, and keyboarding errors. Most word processor software has a spelling dictionary that can be used to verify material. If that is not available, reading from right to left as though you were looking at a spelling list will help.
4. Read *only* what is printed, and not what you *think* is printed.
5. Develop a "mailability" conscience.
6. Correct errors as you reread.
7. Retype if necessary and proofread the final version.

KEY IDEA: STANDARD PROOFREADING SYMBOLS

You should learn the standard proofreading symbols if possible.

FUNCTION	SYMBOL	USE IN TEXT
Align the text	⊔	The ⊔two⊔ nurses
	⊓	The ⊓two⊓ nurses
	[	[The two nurses
	]	The two nurses]
Case:		
Capitalize	≡ or	Drs. Jim and susan (≡ under s)
Uppercase	cap	Drs. Jim and susan (cap)
Lowercase	lc or /	Drs. JiM and Susan (/ through M)
		Drs. JiM and Susan (lc)
Insert:		
Apostrophe	’ over ∨	The nurses pen
Comma	∧ with ,	Bacteria virus and fungus
Dash	∧ with –	We need you now!
Hyphen	∧ with -	Early morning surgery
Letter or number	∧ with s	Bedpan and thermometer
Period	∧ with .	Dr. J Easton.
Quotation marks	∨ with “ ”	I feel ill, Tom said.
Delete	⟋ℯ	Therapist ~~and nurse~~
Delete and add	— or /	Therapist and n/rse (u above)
Delete and close up	(/)	Therapist and n(u)urse
Close up:		
Horizontal	⊂⊃	Therapist and nur se
Vertical	( )	Doctor and nurse ( ) Therapist and aide
Ignore correction	...... or stet	Therapist ~~and doctor~~ (dotted underline)

FUNCTION	SYMBOL	USE IN TEXT
Italicize or underline	ital or ___	The surgery is here.
		The surgery is here. (surgery underlined, marked ital)
Move text	(circle and arrow)	Nurse Brown and Dr. (Brown circled, moved)
New paragraph	¶	Dr. Jon is operating this morning.
Spacing:		
Horizontal	#	Doctor andnurse
Vertical:		
Double	DS>	DS> Dr. Jon is not going to do the tonsillectomy today afterall.
Single	SS>	You can't be sleepy and proofread SS> the material accurately.
Spell out word(s)	sp	Fifth Ave. sp
		sp 5th Avenue
Transpose:		
Letters	(transpose mark)	Doctor
Words	(transpose mark)	Hands must steady be.
Verify accuracy	(?)	The operation is scheduled for (?) 6:00 a.m.

KEY IDEA: FOREIGN SOUNDS IN ENGLISH

Transcribing dictation produced by those who are speaking English as a second language can be quite challenging. It would probably be a good idea to listen through at least one time before beginning to transcribe. Get your ears "tuned" to the different sounds.

Every language has its own set of rules for pronunciation. Since it would be impossible to list all the countries of the world, this list will contain some of the more common ones you will encounter. *Remember that according to their own language rules, they are pronouncing correctly*. You will need to develop listening skills to detect them.

Some languages have no articles; thus, a speaker may drop "a," "an," and "the" before a noun. In other languages an article precedes every noun, so speakers may add them when speaking English.

Word endings such as "*s*," "*ed*," "*al*," and "*ive*" may be dropped. Other word endings not used in English may be heard, for example, abdomen*s* instead of abdomen. Other sounds follow:

1. A final *d* is sometimes pronounced as a *t*.
2. *De* or *ze* may be spoken instead of *the*.
3. The *th* sound is difficult for some and may sound like a *t* or an *s*. *Think* may become *tink* or *sink*.
4. The *g* sound may be replaced by a *k*, resulting in *tinkling* rather than *tingling*.
5. An *l* may be substituted for a *r*, such as *l*eceive for *r*eceive or p*l*esc*l*iption for p*r*esc*r*iption. (Some words with *ch*, *l*, and *r* become very difficult for those speaking English as a second language.)
6. *V* may be pronounced as a *b*.
7. Some Germanic languages pronounce the *c* as a *k* sound; thus the word for *c*ephalic may become *k*ephalic. Other sounds that may be different include: *us* may become *oose* and the short *i* becomes *ee*.
8. Some Spanish speakers may add an *eh* before words that begin with an *s*. Thus, *spend* becomes *e*spend.
9. *X* may become *s*; thus e*x*tension would become e*s*tension.
10. A speaker may pronounce final consonants to have an added syllable at the end, for example, *rest* becomes rest*eh*.
11. *A* is often pronounced *ah* as the first letter is pronounced in Spanish. V*a*sodilator may become v*ah*sodilator.
12. The *ed* endings are pronounced as a separate syllable. *Incised* becomes incise-*ed*.
13. Comma (punctuation) may become *koma* and could be understood for coma.

LEARNING ACTIVITIES

ACTIVITY 8-1

Following are three medical reports that were transcribed from dictation. The transcriptionist has made many errors. Retype the reports as they appear here. Then proofread and correct them, using the proofreading symbols. When you finish, check them with the key and mark any errors in red. You should strive for 100 percent accuracy.

ACTIVITY 8-1a

May 16, 19--

Jack A Randa

History: Reports problems with blured visiion,
onset six-eightt weeks ago.
Exam: Visual acuity is 20/50 in th right eye and
20/40 in the eye. Hyperopic astigmatism was found
andlenses perscribed whcih improve the vision to 20/40
in the right eye and 2025 in the lift eye.
Slight amblyopia right eye,

RX: 1. Leses perscribed.
2. Patch to be worn wver left eye six week.
4. Rechek in six weeks.

Dr. I makem See

ACTIVITY 8-1b

May 16 19--

Ashley Oakes

History: Last seeen sis weeks ago. Had has no
seizures and felt well. Has stumbles too times
recently when triing to step up or step of a curb.
Thinks somethink is wrong with right feet.
Exam: Wt.: 185#; HT.: 5"8'; BP: 140/80.
Neurologicl exam entirety normal. EENT, neck, hart, lungs,
and adbomen entirely norrmal.
Diagnosis: Probable vissual distrubance - problem with
glasses.

rx: 1. Advize have eyes and glasses checked
2. Advises loose weight.
3.Low fat diet givenn.
4. Returm one month.

U.R. Well, MD

ACTIVITY 8-1c

May 16, 19--

Daisy A. Elm

history: Intmittent sesation of pressure in chest for one month. No related to any activity. No S.O.B. and doesnt radiate into either shoulder or arm. Pain is described as being below ther sternum. (Points to arm).
Exam: PB: 172/100; Ht.: 5'3'; Wt.: 145#.
EENT, neck, heart, lung, abdomin, and estremities all esentially negative.

RX: 1. EKg - see report in section lab
2. Atarax 25 mg., Tabs. #100, 1 q.i.d.
3. Returm one week for BP recheck.

H. A. Harms, MD

ACTIVITY 8-2

Write correctly the word that has been pronounced incorrectly. The sound to be changed is underlined.

The nurse had a hart time. ______________________

The patient espired. ______________________

The doctor explain-ed. ______________________

He cut the vagoose nerve. ______________________

The kerebrum (brain) is bruised. ______________________

His hand had a tinkling feeling. ______________________

Ze doctor was late. ______________________

It's polite to use prease and sank you. ______________________

The pharmacist filled the plescliption. ______________________

Quick, there is fetal deestress! ______________________

NOTES

CHAPTER 9

Letter Writing

OBJECTIVES

After studying this chapter, the student will be able to:

1. Identify and distinguish four basic business letter styles.
2. List and explain six criteria used for professional business correspondence.
3. Produce communications with mailability.
4. Create memos and patient report notes that are concise and easy to understand.
5. Explain and use five composition tips in creating professional correspondence.

KEY IDEA: THE IMPORTANCE OF LETTER WRITING

In the tremendously fast-paced, worldwide area of communications, letter writing is one of the most effective methods a person can use. Millions of letters are written daily. Some are friendly and informal; some are extremely formal. There are announcements, promotions, invitations, and there are official letters and various forms of business communication. To transcriptionists, the latter form is the most important, and it is the one we shall discuss in this chapter.

Comparatively few changes have been made in letter writing over the years, except that most letters are less formal than they used to be. Regardless of the form used, however, letters represent the sender. They can present an extremely flattering picture, or a deceptively negative one. Your objective should always be to produce a perfect letter using the following criteria:

1. Appearance—pleasant to look at, like a picture with a gorgeous frame. The only thing outside that frame would be the letterhead.
2. Form—appropriate to the occasion.
3. Wording—straightforward, simple, and understandable; all correctly spelled.
4. Grammar—correct in wording, phrases, and sentence structure.
5. Punctuation—capitalization, periods, commas, and the like, all properly done.
6. Abbreviations—all usual abbreviations spelled out in full.

KEY IDEA: LETTER STYLES

Letter style refers to the way a letter is formatted or "set up" on the page. Although there are older, more traditional formats, they will not be considered here. We shall discuss the most common letter styles in use today: the full block, modified block, modified block—indented, and the simplified letter styles. All of the following information and examples are according to *Webster's Secretarial Handbook, 1990.*

In these styles, most businesses prefer a type of punctuation called mixed or modified punctuation, which appears as follows:

colon	:	follows salutation, reference initials, copies (cc:), and enclosure (Encl:).
comma	,	follows complimentary close

A newer trend, called *open punctuation*, uses no punctuation after each of the above.

Block Style

In recent years the full block form has been adapted by most businesses. It is simple, its appearance is neat, and it is fast to produce.

Block style.

LETTERHEAD	Common Sense Consultants 1041 Hardwork Street Anytown, AS 00002-1234
(3 lines)	
DATE	June 10, 19XX
(3-12 lines)	
INSIDE ADDRESS	Robert Hawthorne, M.D. Make Em Well Clinic 222 Sickly Avenue Anytown, AS 00003-5678
(2 lines)	
SALUTATION	Dear Dr. Hawthorne:
(2 lines)	
BODY OF LETTER	All lines in this letter style are flush with the left margin. It is called a block or full block letter. A variation of this style, the modified block, differs in one respect: the date, reference line, complimentary close, signature, and title are moved to the center point.
(2 lines)	
	Many businesses and professional people use this variation more than any other. Secretaries like it; it's easy to produce, and it looks very attractive. Modified punctuation is used. I would recommend one of the three Block styles.
(2 lines)	
	The salutation, as well as enclosure, copies, and reference initials are followed by a colon. This same style may be used with open punctuation. In open punctuation they are followed by nothing. With mixed punctuation: the salutation—a colon; the complimentary close—a comma; the enclosure—a period; reference initials—nothing.
(2 lines)	
COMPLIMENTARY CLOSE	Very truly yours,
(4 lines)	
SIGNATURE	Sally Secretary
TITLE	Business Consultant
(2 lines)	
REFERENCE INITIALS	ss
(2 lines)	
ENCLOSURE	Encl:
(2 lines)	
COPIES	cc:

Modified block style.

LETTERHEAD	Common Sense Consultants 1041 Hardwork Street Anytown, AS 00002-1234
(3 lines)	
DATE	June 10, 19XX
(3 lines)	
MAILING NOTATION	SPECIAL DELIVERY
(2-3 lines)	
INSIDE ADDRESS	Robert Hawthorne, M.D. Make Em Well Clinic 222 Sickly Avenue Anytown, AS 00003-5678
(2 lines)	
SALUTATION	Dear Doctor Hawthorne:
(2 lines)	
SUBJECT LINE	SUBJECT: Modified Block Letter Style
(2 lines)	
BODY OF LETTER	This is a sample of the modified block style of letter, written with mixed punctuation in the opening and closing lines. This style of punctuation calls for a colon after the salutation and a comma following the complimentary close.
(2 lines)	
	The date, complimentary close, typed signature, and title are again moved to the center point. This differs from the block style, where all of the above are flush with the left margin. All other lines begin at the left margin.
(2 lines)	
	If a subject line is used, it can be either centered over the body of the letter or begin at the left margin. It is located two spaces below the salutation.
(2 lines)	
COMPLIMENTARY CLOSE	Sincerely,
(4 lines)	
SIGNATURE	Sally Secretary
TITLE	Business Consultant
(2 lines)	
REFERENCE INITIALS	ss
(2 lines)	
ENCLOSURE	Encl:
(2 lines)	
COPIES	cc:

Modified block style, indented, mixed punctuation.

```
LETTERHEAD        Common Sense Consultants
                  1041 Hardwork Street
                  Anytown, AS 00002-1234

(3 lines)
DATE                                      June 10, 19XX

(3-12 lines)
INSIDE            Robert Hawthorne, M.D.
 ADDRESS          Make Em Well Clinic
                  222 Sickly Avenue
                  Anytown, AS 00003-5678
(2 lines)
SALUTATION        Dear Dr. Hawthorne:
(2 lines)
SUBJECT LINE           SUBJECT: Modified Block Style
(2 lines)
BODY OF                You have asked us to give you four letter
 LETTER           forms so that you can choose one to use.
                  This is a sample of the modified indented
                  style.
(2 lines)
                       Each paragraph will begin with 5-6 indented
                  spaces. The complimentary close will begin at the
                  center point. The typed signature line and title
                  line are also moved to the center. All other
                  lines begin at the left margin. This modification
                  gives it its name.
(2 lines)
                       Some professionals and business people prefer
                  this style, not desiring either extreme of the
                  simplified or full block. It presents an
                  attractive picture and is fairly easy to set up.
(2 lines)
COMPLIMENTARY                             Very truly yours,
 CLOSE

(4 lines)
SIGNATURE                                 Sally Secretary
TITLE                                     Business Consultant
(2 lines)
REFERENCE         ss
 INITIALS
```

Simplified Style

More modern still is the simplified letter style, also known as the AMS (Administrative Management Society) letter. The salutation and complimentary close are eliminated. The subject line is typed on the third line below the inside address in all capital letters, and replaces the salutation. The sender's name and title are typed three lines below the body of the letter, in all capitals. This letter solves the problem about how to address the person in the salutation. You do not have to worry about whether you are addressing a Miss, Ms, or Mrs., etc.

LETTERHEAD	Common Sense Consultants 1041 Hardwork Street Anytown, AS 00002-1234
(3 lines) DATE	June 10, 19XX
(3-12 lines) INSIDE ADDRESS	Robert Hawthorne, M.D. Make Em Well Clinic 222 Sickly Avenue Anytown, AS 00003-5678
(3 lines) SUBJECT LINE	SIMPLIFIED STYLE LETTER
(3 lines) BODY OF LETTER	Though simplified, this letter is typed in block style with all lines beginning at the left margin. You will notice that it has no salutation and no complimentary close. This saves considerable typing time, and also aids in deciding what is the proper salutation to use (for example, is the lady a Miss, Ms, or Mrs.?).
(2 lines)	Leaving the traditional spacing, the subject line is three spaces below the inside address and the body of the letter begins three spaces below that. Note that the word "subject" is omitted but that all words of the subject are capitals.
(2 lines)	The signature name and title are typed in ALL CAPS four lines below the last line of the body of the letter. Reference initials are usually the typist's only. They are typed two spaces below the writer's name, in lowercase letters.
(2 lines)	In my opinion, this letter is acceptable for business, though more informal than the block styles. I hope that these have been helpful to you.
(4 lines) COMPLIMENTARY CLOSE AND TITLE	SALLY SECRETARY BUSINESS CONSULTANT
(2 lines) REFERENCE INITIALS	cj

Spacing Form for Typed Letters

ALL OF THESE ARE FLUSH TO THE LEFT MARGIN UNLESS OTHERWISE SPECIFIED. SEE SAMPLE LETTERS FOR EXAMPLES OF THE FOLLOWING:

DATE LINE: Three lines below letterhead or on line four, whichever pleases the eye most.

INSIDE ADDRESS: At least 3 to 12 lines below date line, according to the length of the letter. It should consist of two or more lines, with all lines spelled out, and be typed exactly as it appears on the letterhead (of the person to whom the letter is to be sent) if available. Two-letter state designations should be used.

ATTENTION LINE (not always used): If there is one, *two lines below inside address.*

SALUTATION OR GREETING: Two lines below attention line, or inside address, if no attention line. This is omitted in the simplified letter.

SUBJECT LINE: May be typed flush, indented, or centered, two lines below salutation. Not all letters have subject lines. They may be typed in all capitals, with or without the word *subject.*

BODY OF LETTER: Two lines below subject line, or if there is none, two lines below greeting or salutation. *Two lines between paragraphs,* even if letter is double-spaced.

COMPLIMENTARY CLOSE: Two lines below body of letter. Placement depends on style of letter used. See examples on previous pages. If company name is a part of the signature, it is typed in all capitals, two spaces below the complimentary closing.

TYPEWRITTEN SIGNATURE: Four lines below the complimentary close, or the company name. *If the letter is unusually short, place on the sixth to eighth line below* company name or complimentary closing.

TITLE: One line below typed signature, or on the same line as the signature, whichever gives a better balance to the letter. In the simplified letter, type the writer's name and title on the fifth and sixth lines below the body of the letter.

REFERENCE INITIALS: Two lines below signature title. There may be two sets of initials, the first being the author of the document, the second being the typist. Many firms prefer only the typist's initials. Either way is correct.

ENCLOSURE: Two lines below reference initials, and flush with left margin. If more than one, indicate the number enclosed in parentheses.

COPY NOTATION: You never send out a letter without keeping a copy of it for your record. If copies are prepared for the information of other persons than the addressee, the notation "cc:" is followed by the name or names of the person or persons. If more than one person, each should be listed either in alphabetic, or rank order.

MAILING NOTATION: Any special mailing notation (airmail, and the like) should be *typed between the date and the inside address*, flush with the left margin.

SECOND PAGE HEADING: Three bits of information are needed: NAME OF THE ADDRESSEE, PAGE NUMBER, AND DATE, *typed on the seventh line* from the top.

Example:
Robert Hawthorne, M.D. Page 2 June 10, 19XX
Exception— full block format is as follows:
Robert Hawthorne, M.D.
Page 2
June 10, 19XX

KEY IDEA: ADDITIONAL TIPS

TITLES: *No space between periods*— M.D., not M. D.

DATE: *Spell out month*— February, not Feb. Space after comma— February 6, 19XX, not February 6,19XX

PERIODS: At the end of a sentence, followed by two spaces— Thank you for your interest. Please call us.

COLON: Followed by two spaces— Encl: Medical Records.

PARAGRAPHS: *Each paragraph must have at least two sentences.* Each letter must have at least two paragraphs. Exception: the last paragraph before the complimentary closing may contain only one sentence.

KEY IDEA: ENVELOPES

With the advent of the post office optical character readers (OCRs), the addressing of an envelope became more important than ever. The readers are programmed to scan a specific area of the envelope. The U.S. Postal Service asks that you use all capital letters and no punctuation in the envelope address. *The address must be completely within the read zone, blocked and single-spaced.* The two-letter abbreviations for states should be used, along with the nine-digit ZIP codes.

The two standard-sized envelopes are

The #6-3/4 envelope (measuring 6-½ × 3-⅝ in.)
The #10 envelope (measuring 9-½ × 4-⅛ in.)

On the small envelope start the address on line 12, from the top edge of the envelope and 2-½ in. from the left edge. On the large envelope the address should begin on line 14 from the top edge, and four inches from the left.

Sample: #6-3/4 envelope.

```
(2 lines)
   COMMON SENSE CONSULTANTS
   1041 HARDWORK STREET
   ANYTOWN, AS 00002-1234
(indent 3 spaces)                                  SPECIAL DELIVERY
(3 lines down)                                   (5-6 spaces from edge)
PERSONAL



                              ROBERT HAWTHORNE, M.D.
(2-½ in. from edge)           MAKE EM WELL CLINIC
                              222 SICKLY AVENUE
                              ANYTOWN, AS 00003-5678
```

NOTE: Must use two-letter abbreviation for state. The OCR scanner does not recognize state names spelled out in full and those will have to be hand-processed.

Sample: #10 envelope.

```
(2 lines)
   COMMON SENSE CONSULTANTS
   1041 HARDWORK STREET
   ANYTOWN, AS 00002-1234
(indent 3 spaces)                                  NIGHT LETTER
(3 lines down)                                   (5-6 spaces from edge)
   PERSONAL

                              (14 lines down from top)



(4 in. from edge)                        ROBERT HAWTHORNE, M.D.
                                         MAKE EM WELL CLINIC
                                         222 SICKLY AVENUE
                                         ANYTOWN, AS 00003-5678
```

All special notations to the addressee should be typed in all capitals, three lines below the return address. Special mailing notations should be typed below the stamp, all capitals, and end 5–6 spaces from the right envelope edge.

Return addresses are to be typed, all capitals, and begin on the second line from the top edge and three spaces from the left edge.

Traditional addressing in capitalized only form, still single-spaced, but containing punctuation may still be used. However, the U.S. Postal Service prefers the one that the optical character reader can scan. This method also speeds delivery because it can be processed faster.

KEY IDEA: OTHER FORMS

Other communications you may be called upon to type would be letters of appreciation, requests, granting or refusing speaking engagements or other appointments, inner-office memos, and transcripts. These are all in addition to the usual medical reports, radiology or test reports, physical examinations or consultations, according to your employer's occupation or specialty.

KEY IDEA: DIRECTED COMPOSITION

Composing a letter is not easy for many people. In order for you to understand how much thought may go into a letter, you are to compose four of your own. Tips for your composition follow:

Consider receiver: The first consideration is the person who will receive your letter. How much do you know about that person? How busy is he or she? Will he or she welcome your communication? How can you "hook" him or her into reading all you have to say?

Reason clear: Be certain you know the reason you are writing. (Why not call instead?) Also, be certain that the person receiving your letter understands why it was written.

Outline: Outline your thoughts briefly. Read over your outline to make sure that you have all the necessary items, that everything is pertinent and related.

Rough draft: Make a rough draft, typed, and set up in the form of your choice. Look at it as though you had received it. Would you be impressed?

Finished product: Proofread and correct your rough draft. When that is done, type your finished product. Proofread before removing it from your machine. Correct if necessary. Remove and sign it. Make a copy for your files. *Never* send anything out without making a copy. Additionally, type a sample of a #10 envelope, U.S. Postal Service recommended style.

LEARNING ACTIVITIES

Turn in your outline, rough draft, and finished product, along with an envelope for each of the following letters. Use mixed punctuation with each.

ACTIVITY 9-1

(Block Style) Suppose that a law requiring the use of seat belts has not been passed. You work in an emergency center. You are very much in favor of their use. You are writing your representatives in Congress, giving your arguments why they should be used. Compose a brief letter of two or more paragraphs.

ACTIVITY 9-2

(Modified Block Style) You are a doctor of gynecology. You have a patient who has had a positive pap smear (test for cervical cancer). She has not kept her appointment, as instructed, for a repeat in three months. Stress the importance of her return and set another date for her.

ACTIVITY 9-3

(Modified Block Style) You are an administrative medical assistant. A patient has written you complaining about what she feels are excessive charges on her bill. She has apparently forgotten about some lab work that was done.

ACTIVITY 9-4

Using the situation in Activity 9-3, type a letter in simplified style.

NOTES

CHAPTER 10

Medical Terminology Review

OBJECTIVES

Being a Medical Clerical Worker has a chapter on medical terminology. After reviewing that chapter, this chapter, and Appendices A, B, and C, the student should be able to:

1. Define the five word elements that are the basis of all medical treatment.
2. Translate standard abbreviations.
3. Form words using the five word elements.
4. Define words not in Appendices A–C by using *word elements* found there.
5. Explain general guidelines for pronunciation.
6. Demonstrate how some medical words are pluralized.

KEY TERMS

Adjective a word used with a noun that changes its meaning.
Combining form created when a combining vowel is joined to another word element.
Interpret tell the meaning of, explain.
Diphthong the blend of two vowel sounds in one syllable.

Noun a word giving the name of a person, place, or thing.

Plural denotes more than one.

Prefix a letter or group of letters placed before the root which alters the meaning.

Pronounce to say audibly.

Root main part of a word with primary meaning of the word as a whole. Can stand alone.

Suffix letter or group of letters placed at the end of a word; alters the meaning.

Syllable two or more letters joined together to form one sound.

Vowel *a, e, i, o, u* and sometimes *y*. May be used as a combining vowel.

KEY IDEA: BUILDING VOCABULARY

Medical terminology is the basic language of the transcriber. You must learn to use it as fluently as you do you own native language. It is hoped that you have been building your medical vocabulary and adding to your notebook the new words and terms you have been learning. In essence, you will be building your own dictionary with references that will be helpful as long as you are in the medical field. This chapter will be an additive and supplement to the material in *Being a Medical Clerical Worker*. You will be reviewing the old and adding the new.

KEY IDEA: HOW TO BUILD

Just as a carpenter begins with the foundation when he builds a house, you will begin to build your medical vocabulary by starting with the foundation. Concrete, or a similar material, is used for the foundation of a building. In medical terms that foundation element is called a *root* (or *stem*).

Continuing the comparison, numerous types of building materials are needed to complete the structure. They could be lumber, sheet rock, wire, plaster, shingles, and so on. So, too, in building medical words other materials are used: prefixes, suffixes, vowels, and the like. Just as a building always has a foundation and a roof, so do all medical words. Something always joins the foundation and roof. A combining vowel is the in-between element in medical words. One great difference in the comparison is that the root can *actually* stand alone and give meaning.

KEY IDEA: BUILDING ELEMENTS

Some buildings require using all available building materials; some only two or three. To build a medical word, you may sometimes use all elements; sometimes only two, three, or four. We have talked about the foundation, the root. Let us examine the other elements that may be used to build on the foundation. Let us start with the root for *head* and add the prefix *en*, meaning "in" or "inside."

Example: Root— cephal; encephal— inside the head.

Take the same root and add the suffix *itis*, meaning "inflammation of." Now we have an entirely new word.

Example: *encephalitis*— inflammation inside the head.

Changing elements, we use the combining vowel "o" with the root; and we have a combining form.

Example: *cephalo*— head (usually divided cephal/o).

Note that the basic definition has not changed with the combining form, but if we add another root, it will change the meaning. *Malacia* means "softening."

Example: *cephal/o/malacia*— softening of the head.

KEY IDEA: PRACTICE

For fun and practice, use the following elements to build a few words:

Roots: cephal (head), cardi (heart), gastr (stomach).
Prefix: en (inside), a, an (without), bi (two, double).

Suffix: pathy (disease), penia (decrease, lack of), ectomy (excise or remove).
Combining form: "o."

Here are some silly possibilities. You think of others. They do not have to make sense; just be able to define them. Divide the word parts with slashes.

Examples: en/cephal/o/pathy— disease inside the head.
cardi/o/penia— lack of a heart.
gastr/o/bi/o/pathy— two diseases of the stomach.

Once you learn how to build words and define them, you can also take them apart and analyze them just as easily. Therefore, you can understand words that you have never seen before.

KEY IDEA: OTHER ENDINGS

Structures are not just built and left— they use additional materials to dress them up and "finish" them. The same is true in medical word building. There are adjective and noun endings, plurals, different pronunciations, rules and exceptions to those rules, and word variations; many additional materials "dress up" the basics. That is why a terminology class is almost always a necessity as a prerequisite to transcription. Certainly it is the best way to begin.

KEY IDEA: ADJECTIVE ENDINGS

Remember adjectives from the grammar chapter? Certain adjective endings mean *having to do with* or *pertaining to.* They are used repeatedly with various roots. Following is a list of those endings and examples of the same being used. The five most often used:

ac— cardi*ac*
al— derm*al*
ary— pulmon*ary*
eal— pharyng*eal*
ic— cephal*ic*

Other less often used:

iac— chondr*iac*
id— ir*id*
ose— adip*ose*
ous— ser*ous*

KEY IDEA: PLURALS

In English, plurals cause practically no problems. Most of the time you simply add an "s" or "es." It is somewhat different with some medical words. Many medical words originated in the Latin language and plural endings are determined by the gender of the word (masculine, feminine, or neuter). You will not have to worry about determining the gender of the word, but you do need to know the basic way to form plurals as given below:

SINGULAR (ONE)		PLURAL (TWO OR MORE)	
a	bursa pleura	ae	bursae pleurae
is	diagnosis	es	diagnoses
um	datum bacterium	a	data bacteria
us	carpus	i	carpi
ix	cervix	ces	cervices
ex	apex		apices

Exceptions are few. They can be entered into your notebook and memorized.

KEY IDEA: PRONUNCIATION DIFFICULTIES

In the chapter on proofreading the origins and sounds of languages were discussed. Unless you practice saying words aloud, you will probably continue to feel uncomfortable when trying to say them. Make flash cards for new words and practice them every opportunity you have. Say them aloud and listen to yourself. Most medical terms, including the ones from Latin and Greek, will generally be pronounced the same as English with each letter being pronounced. One problem is to know which syllable to accent. Here are some general guidelines for pronunciation:

1. You seldom ever accent the last syllable of a medical word. Most two- and three-syllable words are accented on the first syllable.
2. Every vowel or diphthong makes a separate syllable.

KEY IDEA: DOUBLE CONSONANTS

In the English language any letter other than *a, e, i, o, u* is a consonant. They, and sometimes *y*, are called vowels. Whenever a double consonant appears at the beginning of a word, the first one is silent. If this same pair appears in the middle of a word, they are both pronounced.

Examples: ptosis (TOH-sis)
blepharoptosis (BLE-far-OP-to-sis)
gnosis (NO-sis)
agnosis (AG-noh-sis)
pneumonia (nu-MO-nee-ah)
dyspnea (DISP-nee-ah)

KEY IDEA: CONSONANT COMBINATIONS

Certain consonants can fool you if you do not know they can be different. Some of them follow, with an example for each one:

ch— often pronounced like *k*— chiro (KI- ro), cheilo (KEE-lo)
ph— sounds like *f*— philo (FI-lo), sphygmo (SFIG-mo).
rh— sounds like *r*— hemorrhage (HEM-or-rage), hemorrhoid (HEM-or-roid).

KEY IDEA: LETTERS C AND A

When *c* is followed by an *e, i,* or *y*, it is given the soft sound of *s*; and *g* takes the soft sound of *j*.

Examples: cyanosis (SI-an-O-sis)
meningitis (men-in-JI-tis)

When followed by other letters, both *c* and *g* have a hard sound.

Examples: craniectomy (KRA-ne-ek-to-me)
gastric (GAS-tric)

When a double *c* (cc) is followed by an *e*, *i*, or *y*, you pronounce the first *c* as *k*, and the second one as *s*.

Example: staphylococci (STAF-el-o-kok-sigh)

KEY IDEA: VOWELS AND WORD ENDINGS

A combination of the vowels *ae* and *oe* are pronounced as double *e*.

Example: vertebrae (VER-te-bree)

An *i*, used to form the plural ending of a word has the long sound.

Example: cocci (KOK-sigh)

When an *e* or *es* ends a word, it may be pronounced as a separate syllable.

Example: nares (NAR-ez)

KEY IDEA: ABBREVIATIONS

Another thing that is necessary to learn is abbreviations. They are also learned in a terminology class. In Appendix B there are basic examples given, but you will encounter multitudes of others belonging to specific specialties. You can never *know* all of them, no matter how fantastic your memory, but you can constantly add to your own reference list, plus relying on excellent books like the medical dictionary and Sloane's *Medical Abbreviations and Eponyms*. Becoming thoroughly familiar with Chapter 3 of *Being a Medical Clerical Worker* and studying Appendices A, B, and C could be a good basis for growth.

SUMMARY

Medical terminology is the language of medicine. If you want to be an accomplished transcriber, you will become conversant in that language. Pronunciation, spelling, sounds, and abbreviations are all parts of what you need to learn. Writing or typing and using flash cards is a good way to learn any of the things mentioned.

LEARNING ACTIVITIES

ACTIVITY 10-1

Match the word with the proper definition by placing the appropriate letter in front of the word.

___ prefix	a. Created when a combining vowel is joined to another word element.
___ suffix	b. Main part of a word with primary meaning of the word as a whole.
___ root	c. Placed at the end of a word; alters the meaning.
___ combining form	d. Is added to a word element.
___ combining vowel	e. Letter, usually "o," used to join word elements.
	f. Consonant used to join word elements.
	g. Placed at the beginning of a word; alters the meaning.

ACTIVITY 10-2

Form 30 words from the word elements given below. Note that sometimes you will have to add another letter to the vowel. (The roots used are anatomical terms.)

WORD ROOT	COMBINING VOWEL	SUFFIX	PREFIX
aden	o	centesis	a, an
ateri	o	cyte	ante
arth	o	dynia	anti
cerebr	o	ectasis	circum
cheil	o	ectomy	dia
chir	o	genic	dys
gastr	o	iasis	ecto
gloss	o	itis	en
hemat	o	lysis	endo
mast	o	malacia	epi
nephr	o	megaly	hemi
neur	o	pathy	hyper
oste	o	pexy	hypo
ot	o	plasty	para
pharyng	o	plegia	pre
pneum	o	rhagia	retro
splen	o	rhea	sub
thorac	o	sclerosis	sym
uter	o	tripsy	syn

ACTIVITY 10-3

Return to your list of 30 words and give the definitions for them.

ACTIVITY 10-4

1. Name adjectival endings that mean "pertaining to." _____
   ____
2. What two letters sometimes sound like a *k*? __________
3. Which sound is made by the letters *ph*? __________
4. What is the double consonant used in the root "to know"?
   ____
5. When is the first letter in a double consonant silent, and when is it pronounced? __________
   ____
6. Give the plurals of the following singular forms:
   atrium __________
   bursa __________
   focus __________
   crisis __________
   appendix __________
   cortex __________
7. Most two- and three-syllable words are accented on which syllable? __________
8. What does every vowel or diphthong do? __________
9. When *c* and *g* are followed by *e, i,* or *u,* what sound do they take? __________. Give an example of each: _______
   ____
10. Which letters are *not* consonants and what are they called? __________
    ____

CHAPTER 11

The PDR and Other References

OBJECTIVES

After reading this chapter, the student will be able to:

1. Properly identify the different sections of the *Physician's Desk Reference* (PDR).
2. Demonstrate the difference between product names and generic names and when to capitalize medications.
3. Demonstrate when to use *Webster's Dictionary* or resort to sound to look up terms.
4. Demonstrate when to use the medical dictionary and how.
5. Recall where to find names of instruments, diseases, and the like.
6. Correct contextual material that is obviously incorrect (words that have been misunderstood).

INTRODUCTION

This chapter will in no way tell you all you have to know about words, medical or otherwise. The object is to tell you about problems you may encounter and when, where, and how to find the answer. Proper spelling of words can be a problem, no matter how many rules you remember, like "i" before "e" except after "c" and sometimes "w" and "y." Ordinarily you would simply grab a *Webster's Dictionary* if it's not a medical word, and a medical dictionary if it is. Unfortunately, it is not always that easy. If you are keeping a notebook, it is important for you to include any helpful information you find and may have to use again.

Some of the difficulties you may encounter are discussed, and a solution is suggested to eliminate them. Four books are given to serve as your core of reference. Other very helpful references may be mentioned, and a complete listing of references is provided in the appendices.

KEY IDEA: SPELLING

Medical transcriptionists *must* be able to spell correctly. Ever wonder, "Is it congratulate or congradulate? desiccate or dessicate?" There are a number of words that give pause to even the best spellers. The examples given above are two of them. They are called spelling demons and cause you to experience spelling terrors. If you wish to be a transcriber and have a spelling problem, do not despair. There are resources for help. You shall be learning about four of the most useful ones: the English dictionary, the medical dictionary, the *Physician's Desk Reference*, and the *American Drug Index*.

If you aren't sure about how to spell a word, a general rule is: if it's a nonmedical word, use an English dictionary. (*Webster's Collegiate* is great.) If it is a medical term, use a medical dictionary. (*Dorland's Illustrated* is being used for this text.) If it's the name of a medication, use the PDR or *American Drug Index*.

KEY IDEA: PRETEST SPELLING

Pretest yourself with the medical terms below: one of each pair is spelled correctly; one is not. See how many you can recognize and write correctly.

1.	anatomic	anatomac
2.	aceptic	aseptic
3.	chemotherpy	chemotherapy
4.	chloriform	chloroform
5.	cystic fibrosis	cystec fibroses
6.	dissected	dessected
7.	ethere	ether
8.	gangrene	gangreen
9.	metabolesm	metabolism
10.	ovarian	overian
11.	pathological	pathalogical
12.	perniceous anemia	pernicious anemia
13.	practitioners	practioners
14.	proctascopy	proctoscopy
15.	techniq	technique

In the left column, 1, 5, 6, 8, 10, 11, and 13 are correct. The remainder are spelled correctly on the right. Did you have a problem? If the answer is "yes," you need the Learning Activities on spelling at the end of this chapter.

KEY IDEA: DICTIONARY USE

There are some spelling demons that are exceptions to all the rules. (Remember the "i" before "e" except after "c" . . .) For those, you must make a list for reference, memorize them, or resort to use of the dictionary every time you are not sure. To save invaluable time, you should make an alphabetized list as you encounter them, and put them in your notebook.

What do you do when you do not know how to begin to spell the word? Use the sound and try to find it that way. *The Bad Speller's Dictionary* can be helpful here.

The English language has come to us from many sources: the Latin, Anglo-Saxon, American Indian, French, Spanish, Chinese, Japanese, Swedish, German, Yiddish, Italians, and Dutch. There are others also.

The English dictionary will tell you many things except *how* to spell a word. (A sample of the information found in the dictionary is illustrated in Exhibit 11-1.) You can discover the correct spelling, pronunciation, phonetic spelling, derivation of the word, its meaning or meanings, synonyms if listed, and what part of speech it is. In addition, each dictionary has instructions and explanations for *how to use*.

bor·der (bôr′dər) *n.* [ME. & OFr. *bordure* < *border*, to border < OHG. *bord*, margin: see BOARD] **1.** an edge or a part near an edge; margin; side **2.** a dividing line between two countries, states, etc. or the land along it; frontier **3.** a narrow strip, often ornamental, along an edge; fringe; edging **4.** an ornamental strip of flowers or shrubs along the edge of a garden, walk, etc. —*vt.* **1.** to provide with a border **2.** to extend along the edge of; bound —*adj.* of, forming, or near a border —**border on** (or **upon**) **1.** to be next to or adjoining **2.** to be like; almost be [his grief *borders on* madness] —**the Border** the district on and near the boundary between Scotland and England —**bor′dered** *adj.*

SYN.—**border** refers to the boundary of a surface and may imply the limiting line itself or the part of the surface immediately adjacent to it; **margin** implies a bordering strip more or less clearly defined by some distinguishing feature [the *margin* of a printed page]; **edge** refers to the limiting line itself or the terminating line at the sharp convergence of two surfaces [the *edge* of a box]; **rim** is applied to the edge of a circular or curved surface; **brim** refers to the inner rim at the top of a vessel, etc.; **brink** refers to the edge at the top of a steep slope All of these terms have figurative application [the *border* of good taste, a *margin* of error, an *edge* on one's appetite, the *rim* of consciousness, a mind filled to the *brim*, the *brink* of disaster]

Exhibit 11-1 By Permission. From *Webster's Ninth New Collegiate Dictionary*, © 1990 by Merriam-Webster, Inc. publisher of the Merriam-Webster ® dictionaries. Note the many things you can learn in addition to how to spell "border."

KEY IDEA: MEDICAL DICTIONARY

A medical dictionary is a *must* for every transcriptionist (see Exhibit 11-2). Approximately 1000 new medical words are coined each year, so your dictionary should be as current as possible. If yours is more than a few years old, you will find yourself needing to add more and more to your own notebook listing for new terminology.

Every transcriber finds it easier if he or she has had a class in terminology. If you have not, your medical dictionary has a section at the beginning explaining prefixes, suffixes, combining forms, and roots. This section is called "Fundamentals of Medical Etymology" or simply "Medical Etymology." Become familiar with this and all parts of your dictionary.

hypocholesterolemic

hypocholesterolemic (hi″po-ko-les″ter-o-le′mic) pertaining to, characterized by, or producing hypocholesterolemia.

hypocholia (hi-po-ko′le-ah) oligocholia.

hypocholuria (hi″po-ko-lu′re-ah) abnormal reduction in the amount of bile in the urine.

hypochondria (hi″po-kon′dre-ah) 1. plural of *hypochondrium.* 2. hypochondriasis.

hypochondriac (hi″po-kon′dre-ak) 1. pertaining to the hypochondrium or to hypochondriasis. 2. a person affected with hypochondriasis.

hypochondriacal (hi″po-kon-dri′ah-kal) affected with hypochondriasis

hypochondriasis (hi″po-kon-dri′ah-sis) [so called because it was supposed by the ancients to be due to disturbed function of the organs of the upper abdomen] [DSM III-R] a mental disorder characterized by a preoccupation with bodily functions and the interpretation of normal sensations (such as heart beats, sweating, peristaltic action, and bowel movements) or minor abnormalities (such as runny nose, minor aches and pains, or slightly swollen lymph nodes) as indications of highly disturbing problems needing medical attention. Negative results of diagnostic evaluations and reassurances by physicians only increase the patient's anxious concern about his health, and the patient continues to seek medical attention. Called also *hypochondriacal neurosis.*

hypochondrium (hi″po-kon′dre-um), pl. *hypochon′dria* [*hypo-* + Gr. *chondros* cartilage] NA alternative for *regio hypochondriaca* [*dextra et sinistra*].

Exhibit 11-2 Sample from *Dorland's Illustrated Medical Dictionary*, 27th ed. Philadelphia, W. B. Saunders. Reprinted with permission.

Dorland's Illustrated Medical Dictionary has tables and plates that are very useful for anatomic knowledge. If you are using another dictionary, check the index to see if there is a table or listing of muscles, nerves, arteries, and veins. Dorland's also has *tests* listed alphabetically under that heading. Other headings with similar listings are to be found under *Diseases, Positions, Signs, (Symptoms),* and *Syndromes.*

If you run across a descriptive word or term pertaining to a part of the examination and cannot find that word listed, look under the word it describes. The pulse, for instance, has *76* different words to describe what type of pulse it is. Look under *pulse* and find the term. *Paralysis* and many other terms are similar. Many other nouns, like *joint, aneurysm, diabetes, suture, ulcer,* and *treatment,* are listed with adjectives identifying them.

KEY IDEA: DRUG NAMES

The doctor dictates the name of a medication being used in treatment. Problem? Maybe, unless the name is already familiar to you. Drugs have three names:

1. The *product* or *trade name,* which is usually spoken of as the *brand name.* This name is given by the manufacturer and identifies *only their product* (note the circles "R" following the name, indicating it is registered); for example, Tylenol®.
2. The *common* name or *generic name.* This is usually moderately short, but shared with many others; for example, acetaminophen.
3. The *chemical name,* which is usually rather long, giving the complicated formula for the drug.

When do you capitalize? A *brand name* is always capitalized. The *generic* and *chemical names* are not. How can you know which it is? The *chemical name* is readily identifiable. It is the *brand name* and *generic name* that present the problem. Which is it? An illustration with people might help to separate the two in your mind: a girl named Gail Erin Smith. *Smith* would be the *generic name*– one shared with many others. *Gail Erin* would be the *specific (brand) name* given by the manufacturers of that girl, peculiar to her alone, among all the other Smiths.

Where do you find the difference? Help is readily available in the *Physician's Desk Reference* (PDR). This book is available in all physicians' offices. It is published annually by Medical Economics, Inc., in cooperation with manufacturers whose products are described. Supplements are published to update during the year. Currently, this book has seven main sections, with added information on poison control centers and drug overdose management. This is one of the most useful tools in the doctor's office and an invaluable help to beginning transcriptionists. Main sections to present are listed below. The ones marked with asterisks are those most useful to you. (The colors may change).

Section 1 (white) Manufacturers' Alphabetical Index
*Section 2 (pink) Alphabetical Index of Product or Trade Names
*Section 3 (blue) Drug Product Category Index
*Section 4 (light yellow) Generic and Chemical Index
Section 5 (glossy) Product Identification Section
*Section 6 (white) Product Information Section (Treatment)
Section 7 (green) Diagnostic Products Information Section

A

ACES Anti-Oxidant (Bio-Tech) ... *667*
A and D Ointment (Schering-Plough HealthCare) ... ▣
A.P.L. (Wyeth-Ayerst) ... **2361**
◆ A-200 Lice Control Spray and Kit (SmithKline Beecham Consumer) ... **430, 2090**
◆ A-200 Pediculicide Shampoo & Gel (SmithKline Beecham Consumer) ... **430, 2090**
A.R.M. Allergy Relief Medicine Caplets (SmithKline Beecham Consumer) ... ▣
ATP (Enteric Adenosine Triphosphate) (Tyson) ... *2213*
◆ A/T/S (Hoechst-Roussel) ... **411, 1058**
AVC Cream (Marion Merrell Dow) ... **1286**
AVC Suppositories (Marion Merrell Dow) ... **1286**
Abbokinase (Abbott) ... **502**
Abbokinase Open-Cath (Abbott) ... **504**
Abbo-Pac (Abbott) ... *502*
◆ Accutane Capsules (Roche Dermatologics) ... **425, 1815**
Acetaminophen Capsules, Tablets, Liquid (Lederle) ... *1161*
Acetaminophen and Codeine Phosphate Tablets (Roxane) ... *1922*
Acetaminophen with Codeine Phosphate Tablets No. 2, No. 3 & No. 4 (Warner Chilcott) ... *2287*
Acetaminophen w/Codeine Tablets (Barr) ... *635*
Acetaminophen w/Codeine Tablets (Lederle) ... *1161*
Acetaminophen Elixir, Tablets, Suppositories (Roxane) ... *1922*
Acetaminophen Tablets and Caplets, USP (Warner Chilcott) ... *2287*
Acetaminophen Uniserts Suppositories (Upsher-Smith) ... **2266**
Aches-N-Pain (Lederle) ... *1161*
◆ Achromycin V Capsules (Lederle) ... **414, 1164**
Achromycin Intramuscular (Lederle) ... **1163**
Achromycin Intravenous (Lederle) ... **1163**
Achromycin 3% Ointment (Lederle) ... *1165*
Achromycin 1% Ophthalmic Ointment (Lederle) ... *1165*
◆ Achromycin Ophthalmic Suspension 1% (See PDR For Ophthalmology) (Lederle) ... **414,** *1164*
Achromycin V Oral Suspension (Lederle) ... **1164**
Acid Mantle Creme (Sandoz Consumer) ... ▣
Aci-Jel Therapeutic Vaginal Jelly (Ortho Pharmaceutical) ... **1589**
◆ Aclovate Cream (Glaxo Dermatology) ... **410, 1031**
◆ Aclovate Ointment (Glaxo Dermatology) ... **410, 1031**
Acnederm Lotion & Soap (Lannett) ... ▣
Acnomel Cream (SmithKline Beecham Consumer) ... ▣
Acthar (Rhone-Poulenc Rorer) ... *1776*
◆ Actibine (Consolidated Midland) **409, 883**
Actidil Syrup (Burroughs Wellcome) ... ▣
◆ Actidil Tablets (Burroughs Wellcome) ... **407**
Actidose with Sorbitol (Paddock) ... *1617*
Actidose-Aqua, Activated Charcoal (Paddock) ... *1617*
◆ Actifed Capsules (Burroughs Wellcome) ... **407**
◆ Actifed Plus Caplets (Burroughs Wellcome) ... **407**
◆ Actifed Plus Tablets (Burroughs Wellcome) ... **407**
Actifed with Codeine Cough Syrup (Burroughs Wellcome) ... **745**
Actifed Syrup (Burroughs Wellcome) ... ▣
◆ Actifed Tablets (Burroughs Wellcome) ... **407**
◆ Actifed 12-Hour Capsules (Burroughs Wellcome) ... **407**
◆ Actigall Capsules (Summit) ... **433, 2180**
◆ Activase (Genentech) ... **410, 1027**
Acutrim 16 Hour Appetite Suppressant (CIBA Consumer) ... ▣
◆ Adagen Injection (Enzon) ... **409, 940**
◆ Adalat Capsules (10 mg and 20 mg) (Miles Pharmaceutical) ... **419, 1535**
Adapin Capsules (Fisons Pharmaceuticals) ... **943**
◆ Adeflor M Tablets (Upjohn) ... **433,** *2215*
Adenocard Injection (Fujisawa) ... **985**
◆ Adipex-P Tablets and Capsules (Gate Pharmaceuticals) ... **410, 997**
Adipost Capsules (Ascher) ... *604*
Adrenalin Chloride Solution, Injectable (Parke-Davis) ... **1621**
Adriamycin PFS (Adria) ... **559**
Adriamycin RDF (Adria) ... **560**
Advance Nutritional Beverage with Iron (Ross) ... *1917*
◆ Advil Ibuprofen Tablets and Caplets (Whitehall) ... **435, 2310**
◆ Children's Advil Suspension (Whitehall) ... **435, 2308**
◆ AeroBid Inhaler System (Forest Pharmaceuticals) ... **409, 969**
Aerobid (See Forest Pharmaceuticals, Inc.) (UAD Laboratories) ... *2214*
◆ AeroChamber (Forest Pharmaceuticals) ... **409,** *970*
AeroChamber (See Forest Pharmaceuticals, Inc.) (UAD Laboratories) ... *2214*
◆ AeroChamber with Mask (Forest Pharmaceuticals) ... **409,** *971*
Aerolate Jr. T.D. Capsules (Fleming) ... **967**
Aerolate Liquid (Fleming) ... **967**
Aerolate Sr. & Jr. & III Capsules (Fleming) ... **967**
Aerolate III T.D. Capsules (Fleming) ... **967**
Aeroseb-Dex Topical Aerosol Spray (Herbert) ... *1054*
Aeroseb-HC Topical Aerosol Spray (Herbert) ... *1054*
Afrin Cherry Scented Nasal Spray 0.05% (Schering-Plough HealthCare) ... ▣
Afrin Children's Strength Nose Drops 0.025% (Schering-Plough HealthCare) ... ▣
Afrin Menthol Nasal Spray, 0.05% (Schering-Plough HealthCare) ... ▣
Afrin Nasal Spray 0.05% and Nasal Spray Pump (Schering-Plough HealthCare) ... ▣
Afrin Nose Drops 0.05% (Schering-Plough HealthCare) ... ▣
◆ Afrin Tablets (Schering-Plough HealthCare) ... **429**
Aftate for Athlete's Foot (Schering-Plough HealthCare) ... ▣
Aftate for Jock Itch (Schering-Plough HealthCare) ... ▣
Akineton Injection (Knoll) ... **1140**
◆ Akineton Tablets (Knoll) ... **413, 1140**
Albuminar-5, Albumin (Human) U.S.P. 5% (Armour) ... **598**
Albuminar-25, Albumin (Human) U.S.P. 25% (Armour) ... **599**
Albutein 5% (Alpha Therapeutic) ... *588*
Albutein 25% (Alpha Therapeutic) ... *588*
Albuterol Sulfate Tablets (Biocraft) ... *666*
Albuterol Sulfate Tablets (Geneva) ... *1030*
Albuterol Sulfate Tablets (Lederle) ... *1161*
Albuterol Sulfate Tablets (Warner Chilcott) ... *2287*
◆ Aldactazide (Searle) ... **430, 2052**
◆ Aldactone (Searle) ... **430, 2053**
◆ Aldoclor Tablets (Merck Sharp & Dohme) ... **418, 1366**
Aldomet Ester HCl Injection (Merck Sharp & Dohme) ... **1370**
Aldomet Oral Suspension (Merck Sharp & Dohme) ... **1368**
◆ Aldomet Tablets (Merck Sharp & Dohme) ... **418, 1368**
◆ Aldoril Tablets (Merck Sharp & Dohme) ... **418, 1372**
◆ Alfenta Injection (Janssen) ... **413, 1109**
◆ Alferon N Injection (Purdue Frederick) ... **423, 1743**
Alimentum Protein Hydrolysate Formula With Iron (Ross) ... *1909*
Alka-Mints Chewable Antacid (Miles Consumer) ... ▣
Alka-Seltzer Advanced Formula Antacid & Non-Aspirin Pain Reliever (Miles Consumer) ... ▣
Alka-Seltzer Effervescent Antacid (Miles Consumer) ... **1519**
Alka-Seltzer Effervescent Antacid and Pain Reliever (Miles Consumer) ... **1518**
Alka-Seltzer Extra Strength Effervescent Antacid and Pain Reliever (Miles Consumer) ... **1519**
Alka-Seltzer (Flavored) Effervescent Antacid and Pain Reliever (Miles Consumer) ... **1518**
Alka-Seltzer Plus Cold Medicine (Miles Consumer) ... ▣
Alka-Seltzer Plus Night-Time Cold Medicine (Miles Consumer) ... ▣
◆ Alkeran (Burroughs Wellcome) ... **407, 747**
Allbee with C Caplets (A.H. Robins) ... ▣
Allbee C-800 Plus Iron Tablets (A.H. Robins) ... ▣
Allbee C-800 Tablets (A.H. Robins) ... ▣
Allent Capsules (Ascher) ... *604*

(◆ **Shown in Product Identification Section**) *Italic Page Number* **Indicates Brief Listing** (▣ **Described in PDR For Nonprescription Drugs**)

Exhibit 11-3 Sample from PDR Section 2—Alphabetical Index of Product or Trade Names. Copyright © *Physicians' Desk Reference*, 1991 edition, published by Medical Economics Data, Oradell, NJ 07649.

A

ACE INHIBITORS
(see under CARDIOVASCULAR PREPARATIONS)

AIDS CHEMOTHERAPEUTIC AGENTS
Retrovir Capsules (Burroughs Wellcome) **407, 788**
Retrovir I.V. Infusion (Burroughs Wellcome) **791**
Retrovir Syrup (Burroughs Wellcome) **788**

AIDS RELATED COMPLEX (ARC) THERAPEUTIC AGENTS
Bactrim DS Tablets (Roche) **425, 1828**
Bactrim I.V. Infusion (Roche) **1826**
Bactrim Pediatric Suspension (Roche) **1828**
Bactrim Suspension (Roche) **1828**
Bactrim Tablets (Roche) **425, 1828**
Intron A (Schering) **1998**
NebuPent for Inhalation Solution (Lyphomed Division of Fujisawa) **1275**
Pentam 300 (Lyphomed Division of Fujisawa) **1276**
Retrovir Capsules (Burroughs Wellcome) **407, 788**
Retrovir I.V. Infusion (Burroughs Wellcome) **791**
Retrovir Syrup (Burroughs Wellcome) **788**
Roferon-A Injection (Roche) **1853**

ACNE PRODUCTS
(see under DERMATOLOGICALS, ACNE PREPARATIONS)

ADHESION BARRIER
Interceed (TC7) Absorbable Adhesion Barrier (Johnson & Johnson Medical) **1125**

ADRENAL CORTICAL STEROID INHIBITOR
Cytadren (CIBA Pharmaceutical) **408, 848**

ADRENAL CORTICOSTEROID
Pediapred Oral Liquid (Fisons Pharmaceuticals) **959**

ALCOHOL ABUSE REDUCTION PREPARATIONS
Antabuse Tablets (Wyeth-Ayerst) **436, 2358**

ALLERGENS
Allergenic Extracts, Diagnosis and/or Immunotherapy

ANALGESICS

ACETAMINOPHEN
Datril Extra-Strength Analgesic Tablets (Bristol-Myers Products) **407, 742**

ACETAMINOPHEN & COMBINATIONS
Acetaminophen Uniserts Suppositories (Upsher-Smith) **2266**
Anacin-3 Children's Acetaminophen Chewable Tablets, Alcohol-Free Liquid, and Infants' Drops (Whitehall) **435, 2311**
Anacin-3 Maximum Strength Acetaminophen Film Coated Caplets (Whitehall) **435, 2311**
Anacin-3 Maximum Strength Acetaminophen Film Coated Tablets (Whitehall) **435, 2311**
Anacin-3 Regular Strength Acetaminophen Film Coated Tablets (Whitehall) **435, 2311**
Anexsia 5/500 (Beecham Laboratories) **405, 641**
Anexsia 7.5/650 (Beecham Laboratories) **405, 642**
Allergy Sinus Comtrex Multi-Symptom Allergy/Sinus Formula Tablets & Caplets (Bristol-Myers Products) **407, 741**
Cough Formula Comtrex (Bristol-Myers Products) **741**
Comtrex Multi-Symptom Cold Reliever Tablets/Caplets/Liqui-Gels/Liquid (Bristol-Myers Products) **407, 740**
Congespirin For Children Aspirin Free Chewable Cold Tablets (Bristol-Myers Products) **742**
Dristan Decongestant/Antihistamine/Analgesic Coated Caplets (Whitehall) **435, 2314**
Dristan Decongestant/Antihistamine/Analgesic Coated Tablets (Whitehall) **435, 2314**
Maximum Strength Dristan Decongestant/Analgesic Coated Caplets (Whitehall) **435, 2314**
DuoCet (Mason) **417, 1319**
Esgic-Plus Tablets (Forest Pharmaceuticals) **409, 981**
Esgic Tablets & Capsules (Forest Pharmaceuticals) **409, 980**
Aspirin Free Excedrin (Bristol-Myers Products) **407, 742**
Excedrin Extra-Strength Analgesic Tablets & Caplets (Bristol-Myers Products) **407, 742**
Excedrin P.M. Analgesic/Sleeping Aid

Talacen (Winthrop Pharmaceuticals) **436, 2350**
Tylenol acetaminophen Children's Chewable Tablets & Elixir (McNeil Consumer) **417, 1327**
Tylenol Allergy Sinus Medication Caplets, Maximum Strength (McNeil Consumer) **417, 1332**
Tylenol with Codeine Phosphate Elixir (McNeil Pharmaceutical) **418, 1341**
Tylenol with Codeine Phosphate Tablets (McNeil Pharmaceutical) **418, 1341**
Tylenol, Extra-Strength, acetaminophen Adult Liquid Pain Reliever (McNeil Consumer) **1328**
Tylenol, Extra-Strength, acetaminophen Caplets, Gelcaps, Tablets (McNeil Consumer) **417, 1328**
Tylenol, Infants' Drops (McNeil Consumer) **417, 1327**
Tylenol, Junior Strength, acetaminophen Coated Caplets, Grape Chewable Tablets (McNeil Consumer) **417, 1327**
Tylenol, Regular Strength, acetaminophen Tablets and Caplets (McNeil Consumer) **417, 1328**
Tylox Capsules (McNeil Pharmaceutical) **418, 1342**
Vicodin (Knoll) **413, 1156**
Vicodin ES Tablets (Knoll) **413, 1158**
Wygesic Tablets (Wyeth-Ayerst) **438, 2466**
Zydone Capsules (DuPont Multi-Source Products) **410, 919**

ASPIRIN
Arthritis Strength Bufferin Analgesic Caplets (Bristol-Myers Products) **407, 740**
Extra Strength Bufferin Analgesic Tablets (Bristol-Myers Products) **407, 740**
Bufferin Analgesic Tablets and Caplets (Bristol-Myers Products) **407, 739**
Easprin (Parke-Davis) **422, 1650**
Ecotrin Enteric Coated Aspirin Maximum Strength Tablets and Caplets (SmithKline Beecham Consumer) **2091**
Ecotrin Enteric Coated Aspirin Regular Strength Tablets and Caplets (SmithKline Beecham Consumer) **2091**

ASPIRIN COMBINATIONS
Anacin Analgesic Coated Caplets (Whitehall) **435, 2311**
Anacin Analgesic Coated Tablets (Whitehall) **435, 2311**

Arthritis Pain Formula By the Makers of Anacin Analgesic Tablets and Caplets (Whitehall) **435, 2312**

ASPIRIN WITH CODEINE
Empirin with Codeine (Burroughs Wellcome) **407, 756**

IBUPROFEN
(see under ANALGESICS, NSAIDS)

NSAIDS
Advil Ibuprofen Tablets and Caplets (Whitehall) **435, 2310**
Children's Advil Suspension (Whitehall) **435, 2308**
Anaprox and Anaprox DS Tablets (Syntex) **433, 2188**
CoAdvil (Whitehall) **435, 2312**
Meclomen (Parke-Davis) **422, 1670**
Medipren ibuprofen Caplets and Tablets (McNeil Consumer) **417, 1323**
Motrin Tablets (Upjohn) **434, 2246**
Nalfon Pulvules & Tablets (Dista) **409, 900**
Naprosyn Suspension (Syntex) **433, 2203**
Naprosyn Tablets (Syntex) **433, 2203**
Nuprin Ibuprofen/Analgesic Tablets & Caplets (Bristol-Myers Products) **407, 744**
PediaProfen Suspension (McNeil Consumer) **417, 1324**
Ponstel (Parke-Davis) **422, 1689**
Rufen Tablets (Boots Pharmaceuticals) **406, 685**
Toradol IM Injection (Syntex) **433, 2207**

NARCOTIC AGONIST-ANTAGONIST
Buprenex Injectable (Norwich Eaton) **1567**
Nubain Injection (DuPont Multi-Source Products) **409, 914**
Stadol (Bristol Laboratories) **718**
Talacen (Winthrop Pharmaceuticals) **436, 2350**
Talwin Ampuls (Winthrop Pharmaceuticals) **2352**
Talwin Carpuject (Winthrop Pharmaceuticals) **2352**
Talwin Compound (Winthrop Pharmaceuticals) **2353**
Talwin Injection (Winthrop Pharmaceuticals) **2352**
Talwin Nx (Winthrop Pharmaceuticals) **436, 2353**

NARCOTICS, SYNTHETICS & COMBINATIONS
Alfenta Injection (Janssen) **413, 1109**
Anexsia 5/500 (Beecham Laboratories) **405, 641**
Anexsia 7.5/650 (Beecham Laboratories) **405, 642**
Astramorph/PF Injection, USP (Preservative-Free) (Astra) **605**

Exhibit 11-4 Sample from PDR Section 3—Drug Product Category Index. Copyright © *Physicians' Desk Reference*, 1991 edition, published by Medical Economics Data, Oradell, NJ 07649.

It is a good idea to become familiar with at least the sections marked with asterisks. Here is how you might use them:

When you hear the name of the dictated medicine, check *first* in the alphabetical *Product Name Section*. If you find it there, you *always capitalize* it, with few exceptions, such as pHisoHex. Be certain to type any exception just as it appears in the PDR.

If the name is not in the alphabetical index, check the generic and chemical section (Exhibit 11-5). If it is there, you do not capitalize. If you know the product name and wish to look up the generic, do so by turning to the referenced page listed in the alphabetical index. That will take you to Section 5, where you can obtain many different bits of information. The generic name will be listed directly below the brand or product name (see Exhibit 11-3).

Why would Section 3 (see Exhibit 11-4) be useful? If the doctor is dictating about treating infections and you do not

A

ACEBUTOLOL HYDROCHLORIDE

Sectral Capsules (Wyeth-Ayerst) **438, 2444**

ACETAMINOPHEN

Acetaminophen Capsules, Tablets, Liquid (Lederle) *1161*
Acetaminophen and Codeine Phosphate Tablets (Roxane) *1922*
Acetaminophen with Codeine Phosphate Tablets No. 2, No. 3 & No. 4 (Warner Chilcott) *2287*
Acetaminophen w/Codeine Tablets (Barr) *635*
Acetaminophen w/Codeine Tablets (Lederle) *1161*
Acetaminophen Elixir, Tablets, Suppositories (Roxane) *1922*
Acetaminophen Tablets and Caplets, USP (Warner Chilcott) *2287*
Acetaminophen Uniserts Suppositories (Upsher-Smith) **2266**
Anacin-3 Children's Acetaminophen Chewable Tablets, Alcohol-Free Liquid, and Infants' Drops (Whitehall) **435, 2311**
Anacin-3 Maximum Strength Acetaminophen Film Coated Caplets (Whitehall) **435, 2311**
Anacin-3 Maximum Strength Acetaminophen Film Coated Tablets (Whitehall) **435, 2311**
Anacin-3 Regular Strength Acetaminophen Film Coated Tablets (Whitehall) **435, 2311**
Anexsia 5/500 (Beecham Laboratories) **405, 641**
Anexsia 7.5/650 (Beecham Laboratories) **405, 642**
Bancap HC Capsules (Forest Pharmaceuticals) **409, 973**
Butalbital, Acetaminophen & Caffeine Tablets (Geneva) *1030*
Capital and Codeine Suspension (Carnrick) **408,** *821*
Chlorzoxazone with APAP Tablets (Duramed) *935*
Codalan Tablets (Lannett) *1160*
Co-Gesic Tablets (Central Pharmaceuticals) **408,** *830*
Allergy Sinus Comtrex Multi-Symptom Allergy/Sinus Formula Tablets & Caplets (Bristol-Myers Products) **407, 741**
Cough Formula Comtrex (Bristol-Myers Products) **741**
Comtrex Multi-Symptom Cold Reliever Tablets/Caplets/ Liqui-Gels/Liquid (Bristol-Myers Products) **407, 740**
Congespirin For Children Aspirin Free Chewable Cold Tablets (Bristol-Myers Products) **742**
Darvocet-N 50 (Lilly) **415, 1223**
Darvocet-N 100 (Lilly) **415, 1223**
Datril Extra-Strength Analgesic Tablets (Bristol-Myers Products) **407, 742**
Dolacet Capsules (Hauck) *1052*
Dolene AP-65 Tablets (Lederle) *1161*
Dristan Decongestant/ Antihistamine/ Analgesic Coated Caplets (Whitehall) **435, 2314**
Dristan Decongestant/ Antihistamine/ Analgesic Coated Tablets (Whitehall) **435, 2314**
Maximum Strength Dristan Decongestant/Analgesic Coated Caplets (Whitehall) **435, 2314**
DuoCet (Mason) **417, 1319**
Esgic-Plus Tablets (Forest Pharmaceuticals) **409, 981**
Esgic Tablets & Capsules (Forest Pharmaceuticals) **409, 980**
Aspirin Free Excedrin (Bristol-Myers Products) **407, 742**
Excedrin Extra-Strength Analgesic Tablets & Caplets (Bristol-Myers Products) **407, 742**
Excedrin P.M. Analgesic/Sleeping Aid Tablets, Caplets and Liquid (Bristol-Myers Products) **743**
Sinus Excedrin Analgesic, Decongestant Tablets & Caplets (Bristol-Myers Products) **743**
4-Way Cold Tablets (Bristol-Myers Products) **743**
Feverall Sprinkle Caps (Upsher-Smith) **2266**
Feverall Suppositories (Upsher-Smith) **2266**
Fioricet Tablets (Sandoz Pharmaceuticals) **427, 1946**
Gelpirin Tablets (Alra Laboratories) *589*
Gelpirin-CCF Tablets (Alra Laboratories) *589*
Hycomine Compound Tablets (DuPont Multi-Source Products) **910**
Hyco-Pap Capsules (Lunsco) *1275*
Hydrocet Capsules (Carnrick) **408, 821**
Hydrocodone Bitartrate w/Acetaminophen Tablets (Barr) *635*
Hydrocodone Bitartrate w/Acetaminophen Tablets (Geneva) *1030*
Hy-Phen Tablets (formerly Hycodaphen) (Ascher) *605*
Isocom Capsules (Nutripharm) **1582**
Lorcet Plus (UAD Laboratories) **433,** *2214*
Lorcet-HD (UAD Laboratories) *2214*
Lortab Liquid (Russ) **427, 1931**
Lortab 2.5/500 Tablets (Russ) **427, 1931**
Lortab 5/500 Tablets (Russ) .. **427, 1931**
Lortab 7.5/500 Tablets (Russ) **427, 1931**
Lurline PMS Tablets (Fielding) **943**
Medigesic Capsules/Tablets (U.S. Pharmaceutical) *2215*
Midrin Capsules (Carnrick) **408, 822**
Oxycodone w/Acetaminophen Tablets (Barr) *635*
Pacaps Capsules (Lunsco) *1275*
Percocet Tablets (Du Pont Pharmaceuticals) **409, 929**
Percogesic Analgesic Tablets (Richardson-Vicks) **1790**
Phenaphen with Codeine Capsules (A.H. Robins) **424, 1802**
Phenaphen-650 with Codeine Tablets (A.H. Robins) **424, 1803**
Phrenilin Forte Capsules (Carnrick) **408, 824**
Phrenilin Tablets (Carnrick) **408, 824**
Propoxyphene HCl/Acetaminophen Tablets (Geneva) *1030*
Propoxyphene Hydrochloride & Acetaminophen Tablets (Mylan) *1565*
Propoxyphene Napsylate and Acetaminophen Tablets (Barr) *635*
Propoxyphene Napsylate/Acetaminophen Tablets (Geneva) *1030*
Propoxyphene Napsylate with Acetaminophen Tablets (Lederle) *1161*
Propoxyphene Napsylate & Acetaminophen Tablets (Mylan) *1565*
Propoxyphene Napsylate and Acetaminophen Tablets, USP (Warner Chilcott) *2287*
Protid Tablets (Lunsco) *1275*
Redutemp Tab. (International Ethical) *1098*
Repan Tablets and Capsules (Everett) *941*
Roxicet 5/500 Caplets (Oxycodone & Acetaminophen) (Roxane) *1929*
Roxicet Tablets & Oral Solution (Oxycodone & Acetaminophen) (Roxane) *1929*
Sedapap Tablets 50 mg/650 mg (Mayrand Pharmaceuticals) **1322**
Sine-Aid Maximum Strength Sinus Headache Caplets (McNeil Consumer) **417, 1326**
Sine-Aid Maximum Strength Sinus Headache Tablets (McNeil Consumer) **417, 1326**
Sinulin (Carnrick) **408, 826**
Supac (Mission) *1564*
Talacen (Winthrop Pharmaceuticals) **436, 2350**
Tencet Capsules (Hauck) *1052*
Tencon Capsules (International Ethical) *1098*
Tylenol acetaminophen Children's Chewable Tablets & Elixir (McNeil Consumer) **417, 1327**
Tylenol Allergy Sinus Medication Caplets, Maximum Strength (McNeil Consumer) **417, 1332**
Tylenol with Codeine Phosphate Elixir (McNeil Pharmaceutical) **418, 1341**
Tylenol with Codeine Phosphate Tablets (McNeil Pharmaceutical) **418, 1341**
Children's Tylenol Cold Liquid Formula and Chewable Tablets (McNeil Consumer) **417, 1329**
Tylenol Cold & Flu, Hot Medication, Packets (McNeil Consumer) **417, 1330**
Tylenol Cold Medication Caplets and Tablets (McNeil Consumer) **417, 1331**
Tylenol Cold Medication, Fast Acting Effervescent Tablets (McNeil Consumer) **417, 1329**
Tylenol Cold Medication Liquid (McNeil Consumer) **417, 1330**
Tylenol Cold Medication No Drowsiness Formula Caplets (McNeil Consumer) **417, 1331**
Tylenol Cold Night Time Medication Liquid (McNeil Consumer) **417, 1332**
Tylenol, Extra-Strength, acetaminophen Adult Liquid Pain Reliever (McNeil Consumer) **1328**

Italic Page Number **Indicates Brief Listing**

Exhibit 11-5 Sample from PDR Section 4—Generic and Chemical Index. Copyright © *Physicians' Desk Reference*, 1991 edition, published by Medical Economics Data, Oradell, NJ 07649.

understand the name of the antibiotic, turn to Section 3 and look under antibiotics until you spot the name that it sounded like. The Product Information Section (Section 6, see Exhibit 11-6) contains detailed information (provided by the pharmaceutical companies) about each product.

Other helpful information: The PDR lists the injection materials that are used in radiographic procedures, also the brand names of products used for skin tests and laboratory procedures.

Occasionally the doctor may wish to write a drug company for some reason. Section 1 (see Exhibit 11-7) lists the pharmaceutical companies alphabetically. The addresses of current regional and national offices are given, sometimes with the name of the medical director.

For over-the-counter (OTC) drugs, Medical Economics publishes the *Physician's Desk Reference for Non-Prescription Drugs*.

NASE OPEN-CATH is available in single-dose Univial® packages (diluent in upper chamber) in 1 mL and 1.8 mL sizes containing 5,000 IU urokinase activity per mL.

MAJOR USES

ABBOKINASE OPEN-CATH is indicated for the restoration of patency to intravenous (including central venous) catheters obstructed by clotted blood or fibrin. Basically, the use of ABBOKINASE OPEN-CATH includes the instillation into the catheter a volume of prepared ABBOKINASE OPEN-CATH equal in volume to the internal volume of the occluded catheter. Aspiration attempts should then be made at 5 minute intervals. When patency is restored, aspirate 4 to 5 mL of blood and gently irrigate the catheter with 10 mL of 0.9% Sodium Chloride Injection, USP. A second instillation of ABBOKINASE OPEN-CATH may be required in resistant cases.

SAFETY INFORMATION

Avoid excessive pressure while injecting ABBOKINASE OPEN-CATH and vigorous suction when making aspiration attempts. To prevent air from entering the open catheter, the patient should be instructed to exhale and hold his breath during any time the catheter is not connected to intravenous tubing or a syringe. While thrombolytic therapy is contraindicated in patients with active internal bleeding, severe uncontrolled hypertension, intracranial neoplasm or recent (within two months) cerebrovascular accident, intracranial or intraspinal surgery, there have been no reports which would suggest a contraindication for the use of ABBOKINASE OPEN-CATH for intravenous catheter clearance.

PRESCRIBING INFORMATION

ABBOKINASE® OPEN-CATH® ℞
[ab-bō-kī'nāze open-cath]
Urokinase for Catheter Clearance

DESCRIPTION

Urokinase is an enzyme (protein) produced by the kidney and found in the urine. There are two forms of urokinase differing in molecular weight but having similar clinical effects. Urokinase is a thrombolytic agent obtained from human kidney cells by tissue culture techniques and is primarily the low molecular weight form. It is supplied as a sterile lyophilized white powder. Following reconstitution ABBOKINASE OPEN-CATH is a clear, practically colorless solution.

Each ml of reconstituted ABBOKINASE OPEN-CATH contains 5000 IU of urokinase activity, 5 mg gelatin, 15 mg mannitol, 1.7 mg sodium chloride and 4.6 mg monobasic sodium phosphate anhydrous. The pH of ABBOKINASE is adjusted with sodium hydroxide and/or hydrochloric acid prior to lyophilization.

CLINICAL PHARMACOLOGY

Urokinase acts on the endogenous fibrinolytic system. It converts plasminogen to the enzyme plasmin. Plasmin degrades fibrin clots as well as fibrinogen and other plasma proteins.

When used as directed for I.V. catheter clearance, only small amounts of urokinase may reach the circulation; therefore, therapeutic serum levels are not expected to be achieved. Nevertheless, one should be aware of the clinical pharmacology of urokinase.

Intravenous infusion of urokinase in doses recommended for lysis of pulmonary embolism is followed by increased fibrinolytic activity. This effect disappears within a few hours after discontinuation, but a decrease in plasma levels of fibrinogen and plasminogen and an increase in the amount of circulating fibrin (ogen) degradation products may persist for 12–24 hours.[1,2] There is a lack of correlation between embolus resolution and changes in coagulation and fibrinolytic assay results.

Information is incomplete about the pharmacokinetic properties in man. Urokinase administered by intravenous infusion is cleared rapidly by the liver. The serum half-life in man is 20 minutes or less. Patients with impaired liver function (e.g., cirrhosis) would be expected to show a prolongation in half-life. Small fractions of an administered dose are excreted in bile and urine.

INDICATIONS AND USAGE

ABBOKINASE OPEN-CATH (urokinase for catheter clearance) is indicated for the restoration of patency to intravenous catheters, including central venous catheters, obstructed by clotted blood or fibrin.[3,4,5]

CONTRAINDICATIONS

Because thrombolytic therapy increases the risk of bleeding, urokinase is contraindicated in the following situations:
—Active internal bleeding
—Recent (within two months) cerebrovascular accident, intracranial or intraspinal surgery
—Intracranial neoplasm
There have been no reports, however, which would suggest a contraindication for the use of urokinase for I.V. catheter clearance.

WARNINGS

Excessive pressure should be avoided when ABBOKINASE is injected into the catheter. Such force could cause rupture of the catheter or expulsion of the clot into the circulation. During attempts to determine catheter occlusion, vigorous suction should not be applied due to possible damage to the vascular wall or collapse of soft-wall catheters.

Catheters may be occluded by substances other than fibrin clots, such as drug precipitates. ABBOKINASE is not effective in such cases and there is the possibility that the substances may be forced into the vascular system.

PRECAUTIONS

Carcinogenicity: Adequate data is not available on the long-term potential for carcinogenicity in animals or humans.

Pregnancy: Pregnancy category B. Reproduction studies have been performed in mice and rats at doses up to 1,000 times the human therapeutic dose and have revealed no evidence of impaired fertility or harm to the fetus due to urokinase. There are, however, no adequate and well-controlled studies in pregnant women. Because animal reproduction studies are not always predictive of human response, this drug should be used during pregnancy only if clearly needed.

Nursing Mothers: It is not known whether this drug is excreted in human milk. Because many drugs are excreted in human milk, caution should be exercised when urokinase is administered to a nursing woman.

Pediatric Use: Safety and effectiveness in children have not been established.

ADVERSE REACTIONS

Although there have been no adverse reactions reported as a result of using ABBOKINASE for the removal of clot obstruction from I.V. catheters, the possibility of reactions should nevertheless be considered. The following reactions have been associated with ABBOKINASE in doses recommended for lysis of pulmonary embolism.

Bleeding: The type of bleeding associated with thrombolytic therapy can be placed into two broad categories:
—Superficial or surface bleeding, observed mainly at invaded or disturbed sites (e.g., venous cutdowns, arterial punctures, sites of recent surgical intervention, etc.).
—Internal bleeding, involving, e.g., the gastrointestinal tract, genitourinary tract, vagina, or intramuscular, retroperitoneal, or intracerebral sites.

Several fatalities due to cerebral or retroperitoneal hemorrhage have occurred during thrombolytic therapy.

Should serious bleeding occur, urokinase infusion should be discontinued and, if necessary, blood loss and reversal of the bleeding tendency can be effectively managed with whole blood (fresh blood preferable), packed red blood cells and cryoprecipitate or fresh frozen plasma. Dextran should not be used. Although the use of aminocaproic acid (ACA, AMICAR®) in humans as an antidote for urokinase has not been documented, it may be considered in an emergency situation.

Allergic Reactions: *In vitro* tests with urokinase, as well as intradermal tests in humans, gave no evidence of induced antibody formation. Relatively mild allergic type reactions, e.g., bronchospasm and skin rash, have been reported rarely. When such reactions occur, they usually respond to conventional therapy.

Fever: Febrile episodes have occurred in approximately 2–3% of treated patients. A cause and effect relationship has not been established. Symptomatic treatment with acetaminophen is usually sufficient to alleviate discomfort. Aspirin is not recommended.

DOSAGE AND ADMINISTRATION

CONTAINS NO PRESERVATIVE.
USE IMMEDIATELY AFTER RECONSTITUTION. DISCARD ANY UNUSED PORTION.

Preparation of Solution: *Univial:*

1. Remove protective cap. Turn plunger-stopper a quarter turn and press to force diluent into lower chamber.
2. Roll and tilt to effect solution. Use only a clear, colorless solution.
3. Sterilize top of stopper with a suitable germicide.
4. Insert needle through the center of stopper until tip is barely visible. Withdraw dose.

It is recommended that vigorous shaking be avoided during reconstitution; roll and tilt to enhance reconstitution.

Parenteral drug products should be inspected visually for particulate matter and discoloration prior to administration, whenever solution and container permit.

ADMINISTRATION

When the following procedure is used to clear a central venous catheter, the patient should be instructed to exhale and hold his breath any time the catheter is not connected to I.V. tubing or a syringe. This is to prevent air from entering the open catheter.

Aseptically disconnect the I.V. tubing connection at the catheter hub and attach an empty 10 ml syringe. Determine occlusion of the catheter by *gently* attempting to aspirate blood from the catheter with the 10 ml syringe. If aspiration is not possible, remove the 10 ml syringe and attach a tuberculin syringe filled with an amount of prepared ABBOKINASE OPEN-CATH equal to the internal volume of the catheter. Slowly and gently inject the ABBOKINASE solution into the catheter. Aseptically remove the tuberculin syringe and connect an empty syringe (e.g., 5 ml) to the catheter. Wait at least 5 minutes before attempting to aspirate the drug and residual clot with the empty syringe. Repeat aspiration attempts every 5 minutes. If the catheter is not open within 30 minutes, the catheter may be capped allowing ABBOKINASE to remain in the catheter for 30 to 60 minutes before again attempting to aspirate. A second injection of ABBOKINASE may be necessary in resistant cases.

When patency is restored, aspirate 4 to 5 ml of blood to assure removal of all drug and clot residual. Remove the blood-filled syringe and replace it with a 10 ml syringe filled with 0.9% Sodium Chloride Injection, USP. The catheter should then be gently irrigated with this solution to assure patency of the catheter. After the catheter has been irrigated, remove the 10 ml syringe and aseptically reconnect sterile I.V. tubing to the catheter hub.

HOW SUPPLIED

ABBOKINASE OPEN-CATH (urokinase for catheter clearance) is supplied as a sterile lyophilized preparation in a 1 ml single dose Univial® package (**NDC** 0074-6111-01) and 1.8 ml (NDC 0074-6145-02). Store powder below 77°F (25°C). Avoid freezing.

REFERENCES

1. Bang, N. U.: Physiology and Biochemistry of Fibrinolysis In *Thrombosis and Bleeding Disorders* (Bang, N. U., Beller, F. K., Deutsch, E., Mammen, E. F., eds.). Academic Press (1971). pp. 292–327.
2. McNicol, G. P.: The Fibrinolytic Enzyme System. Postgrad. Med. J. (August Suppl. 5). *49*:10–12 (1973).
3. Hurtubise, Michel R., M.D., Bottino, Joseph C., M.D., Lawson, Millie, R.N., McCredie, Kenneth B., M.D.: Restoring Patency of Occluded Central Venous Catheters. Arch. Surg. *115*:212–213 (1980).
4. Glynn, M. F. X., *et al:* Therapy for Thrombotic Occlusion of Long-term Intravenous Alimentation Catheters. Journal of Parenteral and Enteral Nutrition. *4* (4):387–390 (July/Aug. 1980).
5. Lawson, M., Bottino, J. C., Hurtubise, M. R., McCredie, K. B.: The Use of Urokinase to Restore the Patency of Occluded Central Venous Catheters. Am. J. I.V. Ther. and Clin. Nutr., 9(9):29–30,32 (October, 1982).

Ref. 01-2429-R2

BUTESIN® PICRATE Ointment
[bū'ti-sin pick'rate]
(butamben picrate)

DESCRIPTION

Butesin Picrate is an anesthetic ointment containing Butesin Picrate (Butamben Picrate), 1%.

Inactive Ingredients: Anhydrous lanolin, ceresin wax, methylparaben, mineral oil, mixed triglycerides, potassium chloride, propylparaben, sodium borate, water, and white wax.

INDICATION

For temporary relief of pain due to minor burns.

WARNING

Certain persons, due to idiosyncrasy, are sensitive to this ointment and may develop a rash following its application. In such cases its use should be discontinued, and the ointment remaining on the skin removed with soap and water.

PRECAUTIONS

Should not be applied repeatedly or to large areas except under a physician's instructions. Butamben Picrate stains cannot be removed. Contact with fabrics and hair should be avoided.

DOSAGE AND ADMINISTRATION

Spread thinly on painful or denuded lesions of the skin, if these are small. Apply a loose bandage to protect the clothing.

HOW SUPPLIED

1 oz tube (**NDC** 0074-4392-01).
Store below 77°F (25°C).

Ref. 09-6440-3/R6

Continued on next page

If desired, additional literature on any Abbott Product will be provided upon request to Abbott Laboratories.

Exhibit 11-6 Sample from PDR Section 6—Product Information Section. Copyright © *Physicians' Desk Reference*, 1991 edition, published by Medical Economics Data, Oradell, NJ 07649.

ABBOTT LABORATORIES **403, 502**
For Medical Information
Pharmaceutical Products Division
(708) 937-7069
Hospital Products Division
(708) 937-3806
Order Entry/Customer
Service Inquiries
Pharmaceutical Products Division
(800) 255-5162
Hospital Products Division
(800) 222-6883

Products Described

Abbokinase 502
Abbokinase Open-Cath 504
Abbo-Pac *502*
Butesin Picrate Ointment 505
Calcidrine Syrup 506
◆ Cartrol Tablets 403, 506
◆ Cefol Filmtab 403, 508
◆ Chlorthalidone Tablets 403, *508*
◆ Cylert Chewable Tablets 403, 508
◆ Cylert Tablets 403, 508
Dayalets Filmtab .... ▣
Dayalets Plus Iron Filmtab .... ▣
◆ Depakene Capsules & Syrup .. 403, 509
◆ Depakote Sprinkle Capsules 403, 511
◆ Depakote Tablets 403, 511
◆ Desoxyn Gradumet Tablets 403, 513
Desoxyn Tablets 513
Dical-D Tablets & Wafers 514
◆ Dicumarol Tablets 403, 514
◆ E.E.S. 400 Filmtab 403, 520
E.E.S. Granules 520
E.E.S. 200 Liquid 520
E.E.S. 400 Liquid 520
◆ Enduron Tablets 403, 516
◆ Enduronyl Forte Tablets 403, 517
◆ Enduronyl Tablets 403, 517
EryDerm 2% Solution 518
◆ EryPed Drops and Chewable Tablets 403, 518
◆ EryPed 200 & EryPed 400 .... 403, 518
◆ Ery-Tab Delayed-Release Tablets 403, 519
◆ Erythrocin Stearate Filmtab 403, 521
◆ Erythromycin Base Filmtab 403, 522
◆ Erythromycin Delayed-Release Capsules, USP 403, 523
◆ Fero-Folic-500 Filmtab 403, 525
◆ Fero-Grad-500 Filmtab 403, 525
Fero-Gradumet Filmtab 525
H-BIG *526*
Harmonyl Tablets 526
◆ Hytrin Tablets 403, 526
Iberet Filmtab 528
◆ Iberet-500 Filmtab 403, 528
Iberet-500 Liquid 528
◆ Iberet-Folic-500 Filmtab 403, 525
Iberet-Liquid 528
◆ Janimine Filmtab Tablets 403, *529*
◆ K-Lor Powder Packets 403, 529
◆ K-Tab Filmtab 403, 530
Lidocaine Hydrochloride Injection, U.S.P. 531
◆ Nembutal Sodium Capsules 403, 534
Nembutal Sodium Solution 536
Nembutal Sodium Suppositories 538
Norisodrine Aerotrol 539
Norisodrine with Calcium Iodide Syrup *540*
◆ Ogen Tablets 403, 540
◆ Ogen Vaginal Cream 403, 540
◆ Optilets-500 Filmtab 403
◆ Optilets-M-500 Filmtab 403
◆ Oretic Tablets 403, 543
Oreticyl Forte Tablets 544
Oreticyl Tablets 544
◆ PCE Dispertab Tablets 403, 549
Panhematin 546
◆ Panwarfin Tablets 403, 547
◆ Paradione Capsules 403, 548
◆ Peganone Tablets 403, 551
Phenurone Tablets 551
◆ Placidyl Capsules 403, 552
Quelidrine Syrup 553
Selsun Lotion 553
Surbex .... ▣
Surbex with C .... ▣
◆ Surbex-750 with Iron Filmtab 403
◆ Surbex-750 with Zinc Filmtab 403
◆ Surbex-T Filmtab 403
◆ Tranxene T-TAB Tablets 403, 554
◆ Tranxene-SD Half Strength Tablets 403, 554
◆ Tranxene-SD Tablets 403, 554
◆ Tridione Capsules 403, 555
◆ Tridione Dulcet Tablets 403, 555
Tridione Solution 555
Tronothane Hydrochloride Cream 556

Other Products Available

0.25% Acetic Acid Irrigation, USP (Aqualite)
Sterile A-hydroCort
5% Alcohol & 5% Dextrose Injection
Sterile A-methaPred
Amidate (Etomidate Injection) Ampul, Abboject
Aminophylline 250 mg., 10 ml., Ampul & Vial
Aminophylline 500 mg., 20 ml., Ampul & Vial
Aminosyn 3.5% M
Aminosyn 5%
Aminosyn 7%
Aminosyn II 7%
Aminosyn 7% TPN Kit
Aminosyn 7% with Electrolytes
Aminosyn 7% with Electrolytes TPN Kit
Aminosyn 8.5%
Aminosyn II 8.5%
Aminosyn 8.5% TPN Kit
Aminosyn 8.5% with Electrolytes
Aminosyn 10%
Aminosyn II 10%
Aminosyn 10% TPN Kit
Aminosyn (pH6) 7%, 8.5% and 10%
Aminosyn with Dextrose, Nutrimix Dual Chamber
Aminosyn II in Dextrose, Nutrimix Dual Chamber
Aminosyn-HBC 7%
Aminosyn-PF 7% and 10%
Ammonium Chloride
Anticoagulant Citrate Phosphate Dextrose Solution, USP
Atropine 0.1 mg./ml., 5 ml., Abboject Syringe
Atropine 0.1 mg./ml., 10 ml., Abboject Syringe
Balanced Salt Solution
Bretylium Tosylate in 5% Dextrose Injection (2 mg/mL and 4 mg/mL)
Bupivacaine Hydrochloride Injection, USP, 0.25%, 0.5%, 0.75%, Ampul, Abboject Syringe
Butyn Dental Ointment
Calcijex Injection (calcitriol injection)
Calcium Chloride 10%, Abboject
Calcium Gluceptate Injection Ampul & Abboject
Cecon Solution
Cenolate Ampules
Chromium 10 mL (4 mg/mL)
Colchicine Tablets
Copper 10 mL (4 mg/mL)
Cysteine Hydrochloride Injection
Dehydrated Alcohol Injection, USP
6% Dextran 75 w/v & 5% Dextrose Injection
6% Dextran 75 w/v & 0.9% Sodium Chloride Injection
2.5% Dextrose & ½ Str Lactated Ringer's Injection
5% Dextrose & Lactated Ringer's Injection
5% Dextrose & Ringer's Injection
2.5% Dextrose & 0.45% Sodium Chloride Injection, USP
5% Dextrose & 0.225% Sodium Chloride Injection, USP
5% Dextrose & 0.3% Sodium Chloride Injection, USP
5% Dextrose & 0.45% Sodium Chloride Injection, USP
5% Dextrose & 0.9% Sodium Chloride Injection, USP
10% Dextrose & 0.9% Sodium Chloride Injection, USP
2.5% Dextrose Injection, USP
5% Dextrose Injection, USP
5% Dextrose Injection, USP (ADD-Vantage)
5% Dextrose Injection, USP (Partial fill)
10% Dextrose Injection, USP
20% Dextrose Injection, USP
50% Dextrose Injection, USP
5% Dextrose & 0.15% Pot Chl Injection (20 mEq)
5% Dextrose & 0.224% Pot Chl Injection (30 mEq)
5% Dextrose & 0.3% Pot Chl Injection (40 mEq)
5% Dextrose & 0.225% Sodium Chloride with 0.075% Potassium Chloride Injection (10 mEq)
5% Dextrose & 0.225% Sodium Chloride with 0.15% Potassium Chloride Injection (20 mEq)
5% Dextrose & 0.225% Sodium Chloride with 0.224% Potassium Chloride Injection (30 mEq)
5% Dextrose & 0.225% Sodium Chloride with 0.3% Potassium Chloride Injection (40 mEq)
5% Dextrose & 0.3% Sodium Chloride with 0.075% Potassium Chloride Injection (10 mEq)
5% Dextrose & 0.3% Sodium Chloride with 0.15% Potassium Chloride Injection (20 mEq)
5% Dextrose & 0.3% Sodium Chloride with 0.224% Potassium Chloride Injection (30 mEq)
5% Dextrose & 0.45% Sodium Chloride with 0.075% Potassium Chloride Injection (10 mEq)
5% Dextrose & 0.45% Sodium Chloride with 0.15% Potassium Chloride Injection (20 mEq)
5% Dextrose & 0.45% Sodium Chloride with 0.224% Potassium Chloride Injection (30 mEq)
5% Dextrose & 0.45% Sodium Chloride with 0.3% Potassium Chloride Injection (40 mEq)
10% Dextrose Injection, USP
20% Dextrose Injection, USP
30% Dextrose Injection, USP
40% Dextrose Injection, USP
50% Dextrose Injection, USP
60% Dextrose Injection, USP

(◆ Shown in Product Identification Section) *Italic Page Number* Indicates Brief Listing (▣ Described in PDR For Nonprescription Drugs)

Exhibit 11-7 Sample from PDR Section 1—Manufacturer's Index. Copyright © *Physicians' Desk Reference*, 1991 edition, published by Medical Economics Data, Oradell, NJ 07649.

KEY IDEA: AMERICAN DRUG INDEX

You might find it faster to use the *American Drug Index*, an annual publication that lists both brand names and generic names in alphabetical order. To distinguish between them, the generic names have a bullet-shaped mark (•) in front of them. Drug manufacturers' names and addresses are listed at the end instead of the beginning. Common pharmaceutical abbreviations, table of weights and measures, aid in calculating and converting dosages, and a glossary of commonly used drug terms and definitions are other helps at the end of the book.

Sometimes drug names sound like something else. There are approximately 200 drugs that cause difficulties for pharmacists, either because they sound so much alike, or may look similar when written (examples follow). If you cannot be certain after looking it up, leave a blank, tag that report, and check with the doctor. Do not ever just guess. Remember that these reports must be *accurate*.

Examples: Bentyl and Benadryl; Digitoxin and Digoxin; Gantanol and Gentasol; Haldrone and Halodrin; Urisel and Urised.

Another temporary holdup may be when you understand the doctor to say something that does not make sense in context. Look at your material and think what it should say according to the subject.

Names of instruments, diseases, and the like that have people's names may be found in the medical dictionary, *Merck Manual*, or in another good reference by Sloane for W. B. Saunders, *Medical Abbreviations and Eponyms*. An instrument catalog is helpful also. For radiological terms, W. B. Saunders published another book by Sloane, *A Word Book in Radiology*. Other word books by the same authors are available for numerous specialties.

LEARNING ACTIVITIES

ACTIVITY 11-1

Using the PDR find the generic names for these product names:

1. Datril ______
2. Zyloprim ______
3. Polycillin______
4. Bactrim ______
5. Coumadin ______
6. Sumycin Syrup ______
7. Kenalog 10 (or 40) ______
8. Marax Tablets ______
9. Clinoril ______
10. Gantrisin Tablets ______
11. Azulfidine ______
12. Regroton Tablets ______
13. Novafed A Capsules ______
14. Delta-Cortef Tablets ______
15. Kaon Tablets ______
16. Dexatrim Tablets ______
17. Dimetapp Extentabs ______
18. Cortisporin Cream ______
19. Prostaphlin Capsules ______
20. Metandren Linguets ______

ACTIVITY 11-2

Sometimes you may hear things which simply do not make sense. When that happens, consider the context. What is being discussed?

The following phrases and sentences have been taken from student lessons where tapes were misunderstood. Considering the context, correct the errors so they will read correctly. This activity would probably be best performed in instructor-directed group practice with discussion. The words to be channged are in italics.

1. *CARDIAC:* She had substernal pressure for the first time in her life while shopping, *recarring* on exertion.
2. *EYE EXAM:* There is a deviation of 38 prism *diameters*.
3. *CONSULTATION:* See *adenden* to physical examination.
4. *X-RAY OF LOWER BOWEL:* The appearance of the second portion of the duodenum is consistent with the *resiges* of recurrent pancreatitis.
5. *X-RAY OF LOWER BOWEL:* The possibility of *new plasm* arising in the head of the pancreas . . .
6. *X-RAY OF LOWER BOWEL:* There does appear to be slight *extensive* pressure, . . .
7. *UROGRAM:* An *appendicolic* might conceivably produce this appearance.
8. *UROGRAM:* The visualized lateral contour of the left kidney is faintly *discrimable* and appears normal.
9. *DISCHARGE SUMMARY: PMH:* . . . right wrist carpal tunnel surgery years ago with no *pleasant* symptoms. . . .
10. *PHYSICAL EXAMINATION:* . . . showed an elderly lady who *works a lot* and oriented, and in no distress.
11. *PX EX, SKIN:* There was no *thyroidosis* or edema.
12. *HEART:* . . . with a sinus tachycardia, *weight* 110, Q waves in V, . . .
13. *HEART DISEASE:* a. acute anterior myocardial infarction. b. *pulmonary* artery disease.
14. *BREAST SURGERY:* An incision 6 cm in length was made on the previously marked right *in from* mammary crease.
15. *PRESENT ILLNESS: BABY:* This 2000-gm infant was the product of 30–32 weeks of *ecation* to a 30-year-old diabetic mother.
16. *RADIOLOGY REPORT—KNEE:* . . . *optic* right knee arthrogram.
17. *RADIOLOGY REPORT—KNEE: Holding* shaving and scrubbing of the knee in the usual manner, local anesthesia was infiltrated.

18. *RADIOLOGY REPORT—KNEE: Close laid* ligaments and lateral meniscus appear intact.
19. *PATHOLOGY:* The specimen, *deceived* in Formalin, was labeled . . .
20. *FILM REPORT—KIDNEY:* Impression: *nonfractional* right kidney which appears to be secondary to high-grade destructive uropathy.

ACTIVITY 11-3

Use the medical dictionary for this exercise. Some of the following words can be spelled in two ways; others are misspelled. Correct the list, listing the second acceptable spelling, or if they are misspelled, give the correct spelling. In each situation list the phonetic spelling.

WORD	CORRECT/ALTERNATE SPELLING	PHONETIC SPELLING
1. aneurysm		
2. catalepsy		
3. cesarian		
4. disc		
5. fetal		
6. fontanelle		
7. leucocyte		
8. mammillary		
9. sclera		
10. venipuncture		

ACTIVITY 11-4

The eponyms listed are attached to a test, syndrome, forcep, disease, sign, theory, or part of the body. Use the medical dictionary and fill in the blanks. Number 1 is an example.

EPONYM	ATTACHED TO	DEFINITION OR FUNCTION
1. Banti's	*syndrome*	*congestive splenomegaly*
2. Allbee's		
3. Hodge's		
4. Cushing's		
5. Binet–Simon		

EPONYM	ATTACHED TO	DEFINITION OR FUNCTION
6. Willett		
7. Mantoux		
8. Guillain–Barre		
9. McGill's		
10. Musset's		
11. Strumpell's		
12. Hegar's		
13. Rorschach		
14. Schilling's		
15. Hansen's		

ACTIVITY 11-5

It is exciting to know that facts can be stated in numerous ways. Using an English dictionary, select three *noun* synonyms for each of the words listed.

1. composition ______________________

2. beauty ______________________

3. danger ______________________

4. diety ______________________

5. excitement ______________________

6. impurity ______________________

7. leap ______________________

8. multitude ______________________

9. number ______________________

10. odor ______________________

11. pity ______________________

12. record ______________________

13. sound ______________________

14. thought ______________________

15. use ______________________

CHAPTER 12

Medical Records and Reports

OBJECTIVES

After reading this chapter the student should be able to:

1. List and explain the following transcription reports:
   a. history and physical
   b. progress notes
   c. phone calls
   d. consultations
   e. letters
   f. prescriptions
2. Properly format and type a history and physical.
3. Properly format radiology, pathology, and other medical reports.
4. Distinguish between the kind of typing in a physician's office and various hospital transcripts.
5. Demonstrate the differences in format: full block, modified block, indented, and run-on styles.
6. Demonstrate proper procedure for making corrections.

INTRODUCTION

Transcriptionists work in numerous types of places and will have different types of duties accordingly. We shall discuss two: physicians' offices and hospitals, and the types of transcription in each.

KEY IDEA: PHYSICIAN'S OFFICE TRANSCRIBING

One of the places where a transcriptionist works is in a physician's office. This is an especially good place for a beginning transcriptionist who can perform other duties most of the time. Most individual physicians do not have enough work to hire a full-time transcriber. Clinics, however, may have a central storage area into which all dictation is fed. With numbers of doctors, a full-time transcriber would be needed. Large clinics and health maintenance organizations require numerous transcribers, sometimes maintaining two or three shifts.

What kind of material will you be expected to produce? For physicians there are primarily five: progress notes, consultations, histories and physicals, prescriptions, and phone calls, a sixth being occasional letters. All reports except the history and physical and consultation are typed or word processed one after the other on single sheets of paper, space being left between each patient so that they can be cut apart and taped into the patient's chart. Another similar method is to type or print on continuous-roll, pressure-sensitive paper, which can be cut into small sections and placed in the chart. Others are also on pressure-sensitive paper, but perforated into small sections, easily separated and placed in the patient's chart. They are available at most stationery stores. These are called Time Saver Labels and are exactly that: time saving.

KEY IDEA: PROGRESS NOTES, ETC.

Progress notes are records of the patient's visits, progress, and treatment. Some doctors write in the chart themselves, or dictate to an assistant who writes in longhand on the chart. Those who do not use that method usually dictate on in-office equipment. This dictation must be transcribed and placed into the chart.

The record of every visit must contain certain information, no matter how brief that might be. Necessary information for every visit includes: patient's name, present complaint (why being seen), examination if any, diagnosis if not recorded previously, and any treatment rendered or advised. To prevent any legal difficulties, the originator of every entry should sign or at least initial it.

Any phone call, either to or from the patient, should be recorded. Again, the record can be handwritten or dictated. Prescriptions given at times other than visits are recorded in the same way. A record of a phone call, if handwritten, does not need the patient's name, since it would be dated and recorded directly below the last entry on that person's chart. If the record is dictated, however, the name should be included so that it can be filed in the proper chart. Prescriptions would be entered in the same way. Samples are given for both:

Dictated:

(1) SUSAN ALLBEG
4/6/XX Phone: Pt reports Erythromycin nauseates her; wonders if she can change medications.
Rx: Appt. made to evaluate her.

(2) JESSIE JUSON
4/6/XX Phone to Star Drug: Prescription renewed for Thyrolar-2, Tabs #100, one daily. Ref. 2X.

Written:

(1) Susan Allbeg
4/6/xx Phone: Pt reports Erythromycin nauseates her; wonders if she can change medications.
Rx: appt made to evaluate her.
(2) Jessie Juson
4/6/xx Phone to Star Drug:
Prescription renewed for Thyrolar-2, Tabs #100, 1 daily, Ref. 2x.
SBa

Sample Progress Notes Dictated for Dermatology

Indented style

LESTER COON
4/12/XX
Pt reports no problems.
BIOPSY: Wound left temple area healing well.
DX: Report revealed lentigo maligna.
RX: 1. Referred to Dr. Sinning for extensive removal of near melanoma.
2. Sutures removed.
3. Dry dressing to prevent oozing.

Run-on style

IVA WEATHER: 4/12/XX Pt reports condition is improved. Exam shows only remnants of scaly psoriasis lesions rt parietal area. DX: Persistent psoriasis. Recommended only local treatment with previously prescribed ointment.

KEY IDEA: CONSULTATIONS

Patients who are referred from one doctor to another have reports on consultations sent to the doctor who referred them. They are primarily in block letter style, but may be indented also. Two samples are given for ophthalmology consultations: modified block and full block.

Modified Block

June 19, 19XX

I. B. Goode, M.D.
39 Greenwood Avenue
Anytown, AS 00004-1039

Dear Dr. Goode:

Regarding: Avon Weather

We saw Avon Weather on June 7. There was some question of blurred vision.

At the present time his visual acuity is 20/50 in the right eye and 20/40 in the left eye. EOM balance, media, and fundi are entirely normal. Manifest and cycloplegic refractions were performed, with hyperopic stigmatism found. Lenses were prescribed, improving his visual acuity to 20/40 in the right eye and 20/25 in the left eye. Because of the slight amblyopia in the right eye, the mother was advised to patch Avon's left eye for six weeks, at which time we shall recheck his vision.

Thank you for referring this patient.

Cordially,

I. Makem See, M.D.

IMS:ca

Full Block

June 19, 19XX

I. B. Goode, M.D.
39 Greenwood Avenue
Anytown, AS 00004-1039

Dear Dr. Goode:

Regarding: Avon Weather

We saw Avon Weather on June 7. There was some question of blurred vision.

At the present time his visual acuity is 20/50 in the right eye and 20/40 in the left eye. EOM balance, media, and fundi are entirely normal. Manifest and cycloplegic refractions were performed, with hyperopic stigmatism found. Lenses were prescribed, improving his visual acuity to 20/40 in the right eye and 20/25 in the left eye. Because of the slight amblyopia in the right eye, the mother was advised to patch Avon's left eye for six weeks, at which time we shall recheck his vision.

Thank you for referring this patient.

Cordially,

I. Makem See, M.D.

IMS:ca

KEY IDEA: HISTORY AND PHYSICAL

Histories and physicals are transcribed for both physicians and hospitals. Regardless of the form used, all histories and physicals contain essentially the same information. In physicians' offices they may or may not have forms to be filled in. When they do use forms, they may vary considerably according to the specialty. Doctors tend to evaluate the patients in similar manners, however.

On a first visit the patient is usually asked to give a complete history. That would include present illness and background of it, past medical and surgical history, allergies, and family history. Depending on the type of illness, an examination is performed. A person with foot problems would not expect to have an extensive examination of the chest or abdomen.

Conversely, if a person were anticipating major surgery, all body systems would be examined thoroughly. For surgery, a physician would be required to fill out a hospital form even though the exam and history were done in his or her office. All hospitals use forms. Even though they vary, all require a complete examination and review of all systems. An exception is outpatient surgery, since it is not considered major surgery and would not always necessitate as much detail.

Consultations done in a hospital may be done in a narrative style instead of on forms. Preventive medicine and annual physicals, although extensive, are usually narrative. Each hospital, physician, and clinic will have adopted a standard, using one of the four format styles: full block, modified block, indented format, and run-on. Samples of each will follow. The samples are an annual preventive history and physical. See Figures 12-1 to 12-4.

Although the following include both history and physical, they may be typed on separate sheets of paper, especially if either is very long or detailed.

Full Block

HISTORY

Ura Ben Payne
487 Twosome Street
Anytown, AS 00003-1487
Phone: (060) 123-0090
Birth date: October 3, 19XX

January 18, 19XX

CHIEF COMPLAINT:

None.

HISTORY:

Feels fine but thinks it is wise to have a general physical evaluation.

PAST MEDICAL HISTORY: UCHD. Flu 1984, moderately severe. Received all immunizations, including Tetanus update. Operations—T & A as a child. No injuries, broken bones, and never unconscious.

PERSONAL HISTORY: Single. Works with father in tool and die business. No allergies. No medications.

FAMILY HISTORY: Father and mother both living and well, middle-aged. Older sister and younger brother all good health.

HABITS: Normal bowel movements. Sleeps 7-8 hours/night. Drinks 8-10 glasses water daily. No alcohol. Does not smoke.

SYSTEMS REVIEW:

SKIN: Negative.

HEAD AND NECK: Negative except eyes are myopic. Wears glasses. Denies headaches or visual disturbances.

CARDIORESPIRATORY: Denies all symptoms except becomes short of breath with sudden exercise. Gets no regular exercise.

GASTROINTESTINAL: Appetite excellent. Weight stable. Digestion good. Bowels regular.

GENITOURINARY: Denies nocturia. Urinates several times daily with no difficulty. No history of stones or bladder infections.

EXTREMITIES: No problems.

NEUROLOGICAL: Unremarkable.

Figure 12-1a

PHYSICAL

PHYSICAL EXAMINATION: Height 72 in. Wt. 190# BP 114/80, P 76, regular, T 98.6, R 16. Appears well-developed, well-nourished, white male. Slightly obese.

HEENT: Eyes—positive cover test with latent exophoria. Highly myopic, otherwise negative. Ear, nose, throat—normal. Neck—supple. Thyroid—normal.

CHEST: Clear to A & P. Breath tones normal.

HEART: RSR. No murmurs or adventitious sounds.

ABDOMEN: Slightly obese. LKS not palpable. No masses or tenderness.

GENITALIA: Normal male. Circumcised. Inguinal rings intact.

RECTAL: Sphincter tone good. Prostate—small, nontender.

EXTREMITIES: Negative except several small glomus tumors on fingers.

NEUROLOGICAL: Intact.

LYMPHATICS: Negative.

____

I. B. Goode, M.D.

cs

Figure 12-1b

Modified Block

HISTORY

Ura Ben Payne
487 Twosome Street
Anytown, AS 00003-1487
Phone: (060) 123-0090
Birth date: October 3, 19XX

January 18, 19XX

<u>CHIEF COMPLAINT</u>: None.

<u>HISTORY</u>: Feels fine but thinks it is wise to have a general physical evaluation.

PAST HISTORY: UCHD. Flu 1984, moderately severe. Received all immunizations, including Tetanus update. Operations—T & A as a child. No injuries, broken bones, and never unconscious.

PERSONAL HISTORY:	Single. Works with father in tool and die business. No allergies. No medications.
FAMILY HISTORY:	Father and mother both living and well, middle-aged. Older sister and younger brother all good health.
HABITS:	Normal bowel movements. Sleeps 7-8 hours/night. Drinks 8-10 glasses water daily. No alcohol. Does not smoke.

<u>SYSTEMS REVIEW</u>:

SKIN:	Negative.
HEAD AND NECK:	Negative except eyes are myopic. Wears glasses. Denies headaches or visual disturbances.
CARDIORESPIRATORY:	Denies all symptoms except becomes short of breath with sudden exercise. Gets no regular exercise.
GASTROINTESTINAL:	Appetite excellent. Weight stable. Digestion good. Bowels regular.
GENITOURINARY:	Denies nocturia. Urinates several times daily with no difficulty. No history of stones or bladder infections.
EXTREMITIES:	No problems.
NEUROLOGICAL:	Unremarkable.

Figure 12-2a

PHYSICAL

PHYSICAL EXAMINATION:	Height 72 in. Wt. 190# BP 114/80, P 76, regular, T 98.6, R 16. Appears well-developed, well-

nourished, white male. Slightly obese.

HEENT:	Eyes—positive cover test with latent exophoria. Highly myopic, otherwise negative. Ear, nose, throat—normal. Neck—supple. Thyroid—normal.
CHEST:	Clear to A & P. Breath tones normal.
HEART:	RSR. No murmurs or adventitious sounds.
ABDOMEN:	Slightly obese. LKS not palpable. No masses or tenderness.
GENITALIA:	Normal male. Circumcised. Inguinal rings intact.
RECTAL:	Sphincter tone good. Prostate—small, nontender.
EXTREMITIES:	Negative except several small glomus tumors on fingers.
NEUROLOGICAL:	Intact.
LYMPHATIC:	Negative.

____

I. B. Goode, M.D.

cs

Figure 12-2b

Indented Format

HISTORY

Ura Ben Payne
487 Twosome Street
Anytown, AS 00003-1487
Phone: (060) 123-0090
Birth date: October 3, 19XX

January 18, 19XX

CHIEF COMPLAINT: None.

HISTORY: Feels fine but thinks it is wise to have a general physical evaluation.

PAST HISTORY: UCHD. Flu 1984, moderately severe. Received all immunizations, including Tetanus update. Operations—T & A as a child. No injuries, broken bones, and never unconscious.

PERSONAL HISTORY: Single. Works with father in tool and die business. No allergies. No medications.

FAMILY HISTORY: Father and mother both living and well, middle-aged. Older sister and younger brother all good health.

HABITS: Normal bowel movements. Sleeps 7-8 hours/night. Drinks 8-10 glasses water daily. No alcohol. Does not smoke.

SYSTEMS REVIEW:

SKIN: Negative.

HEAD AND NECK: Negative except eyes are myopic. Wears glasses. Denies headaches or visual disturbances.

CARDIORESPIRATORY: Denies all symptoms except becomes short of breath with sudden exercise. Gets no regular exercise.

GASTROINTESTINAL: Appetite excellent. Weight stable. Digestion good. Bowels regular.

GENITOURINARY: Denies nocturia. Urinates several times daily with no difficulty. No history of stones or bladder infections.

EXTREMITIES: No problems.

NEUROLOGICAL: Unremarkable.

Figure 12-3a

PHYSICAL

PHYSICAL EXAMINATION: Height 72 in. Wt. 190# BP 114/80, P 76, regular, T 98.6, R 16. Appears well-developed, well-nourished, white male. Slightly obese.

HEENT: Eyes—positive cover test with latent exophoria. Highly myopic, otherwise negative. Ear, nose, throat—normal. Neck—supple. Thyroid—normal.

CHEST: Clear to A & P. Breath tones normal.

HEART: RSR. No murmurs or adventitious sounds.

ABDOMEN: Slightly obese. LKS not palpable. No masses or tenderness.

GENITALIA: Normal male. Circumcised. Inguinal rings intact.

RECTAL: Sphincter tone good. Prostate—small, nontender.

EXTREMITIES: Negative except several small glomus tumors on fingers.

NEUROLOGICAL: Intact.

LYMPHATICS: Negative.

____

I. B. Goode, M.D.

cs

Figure 12-3b

Run-On Format

HISTORY

Ura Ben Payne
487 Twosome Street
Anytown, AS 00003-1487
Phone: (060) 123-0090
Birth date: October 3, 19XX

January 18, 19XX

CHIEF COMPLAINT: None.

HISTORY: Feels fine but thinks it is wise to have a general physical evaluation. PAST MEDICAL HISTORY: UCHD. Flu 1984, moderately severe. Received all immunizations, including Tetanus update. Operations—T & A as a child. No injuries, broken bones, and never unconscious. PERSONAL HISTORY: Single. Works with father in tool and die business. No allergies. No medications. FAMILY HISTORY: Father and mother both living and well, middle-aged. Older sister and younger brother all good health. HABITS: Normal bowel movements. Sleeps 7-8 hours/night. Drinks 8-10 glasses water daily. No alcohol. Doesn't smoke.

SYSTEMS REVIEW: SKIN: Negative. HEAD AND NECK: Negative except eyes are myopic. Wears glasses. Denies headaches or visual disturbances. CARDIORESPIRATORY: Denies all symptoms except becomes short of breath with sudden exercise. Gets no regular exercise. GASTROINTESTINAL: Appetite excellent. Weight stable. Digestion good. Bowels regular. GENITOURINARY: Denies nocturia. Urinates several times daily with no difficulty. No history of stones or bladder infections. EXTREMITIES: No problems. NEUROLOGICAL: Unremarkable.

Figure 12-4a

PHYSICAL EXAMINATION:

Height 72 in. Wt. 190# BP 114/80, P 76 and regular, T 98.6, R 16. Appears well-developed, well-nourished, white male. Slightly obese. HEENT: Eyes—positive cover test with latent exophoria. Highly myopic, otherwise negative. Ear, nose, throat—normal. Neck—supple. Thyroid—normal. CHEST: Clear to A & P. Breath tones normal. HEART: RSR. No murmurs or adventitious sounds. ABDOMEN: Slightly obese. LKS not palpable. No masses or tenderness. GENITALIA: Normal male. Circumcised. Inguinal rings intact. RECTAL: Sphincter tone good. Prostate—small, nontender. EXTREMITIES: Negative except several small glomus tumors on fingers. NEUROLOGICAL: Intact. LYMPHATICS: Negative.

I. B. Goode, M.D.

cs

Figure 12-4b

KEY IDEA: HOSPITAL RECORDS AND REPORTS

Many hospital records are handwritten by a member of the medical team, with each addition being signed by that team member. We have covered the history and the physical; now let us discuss other reports generated in various departments of the hospital that are to be dictated and transcribed. Following is a list of reports: discharge summary, operative, radiology, and nuclear medicine (scans), consultation, autopsy, and medicolegal.

A discharge summary is necessary for every patient admitted to the hospital. It is the final progress note and contains the following information: admitting and discharge diagnoses, operation (if any), laboratory and x-ray reports, consultations, course in hospital, and condition at time of discharge. Other items of information included are instructions for follow-up care, medications being taken, therapy, and perhaps date of next office visit. These are dictated by the attending physician or a resident or intern and approved by the attending physician. A copy is mailed to the facility responsible for follow-up care. Two samples are shown in Figures 12-5 and 12-6.

Discharge Summary: Block Style

Enna Fix Dr. P. Dualot

#414360 DICTATED: 8-27-XX

ADMITTED: 8-25-XX DISCHARGED: 8-27-XX

This 56-year-old obese WF with ovarian carcinoma was admitted for her 5th course of combination chemotherapy. Physical examination shortly after admission confirmed the pelvic mass seen on CT scan three months age. She was given her 5th course of triple-drug chemotherapy (Cytoxan,

Adriamycin, and Cis-platinum), to which she responded with only moderate nausea and vomiting. She was thought stable for discharge on 8-27-XX, and so was discharged home to the care of her daughter.

DISCHARGE DIAGNOSIS: Ovarian carcinoma.

PLAN: Surgical resection for residual disease will be discussed with the patient and her family physician, after which further plans regarding future chemotherapy will be made.

ca/8-28-XX

P. Dualot, M.D.

cc: Dr. I. B. Goode
Dr. E. S. Cystic

Figure 12-5

Discharge Summary: Run-On Style

Gussie Glum
#08-05793

Dr. Turnoff
Dictated: 7-24-XX

This 40-year-old WF was admitted with bilateral painful ovarian cysts and pelvic adhesive disease. She underwent exploratory laparotomy and bilateral salpingo-oophorectomy with lysis of adhesions. Pathologic diagnoses were multiple tubovarian adhesions and multiple corpora albicans. Thrombosis of pelvic veins was found bilaterally.

The patient did well postoperatively. She had some separation of the wound edges when the skin staples were taken out. This was treated with daily cleansing with hydrogen peroxide. She was discharged home on otherwise routine precautions. She will be followed in the office in one week. She was given Premarin and an iron supplement.

LT/ca
7-25-XX

Leslie Turnoff, M.D.

Figure 12-6

KEY IDEA: CONSULTATIONS

Consultations are usually written block format, narrative style with consultant's name, patient's name and patient's number (if in hospital), and referring physician's name. Consultations sent for outpatients from the consultant's office to the referring physician have the patient's name, are addressed to the referring physician, and are usually written in a narrative block style (see samples, Figures 12-7 and 12-8).

Hospital Consultation: Block Style

Essie Dublowski	Dr. Fixem
#300466	Dictated: 9-4-XX

TO DR. STEVE SEAMLY:

This 72-year-old Caucasian female saw her LMD regarding complaints of retrosternal chest pain and nonproductive cough. Chest x-ray was suspicious, and she was referred here for further evaluation.

After admission to Anytown General, chest x-ray revealed a lesion in the left mediastinum with some attenuation on the left main stem bronchus. Subsequent bronchoscopy revealed small cell undifferentiated carcinoma of the left lung. SMA profile and physical findings were unremarkable. The patient's disease is thought to be limited to the thorax.

I discussed with the patient at length the nature of her disease and its natural history and prognosis with and without therapy. I informed her that proper therapy would consist of combination chemotherapy and, in the future probably, radiation. The patient was discharged with the understanding that she would consider all that we discussed and return with her final decision regarding treatment.

DISCHARGE DIAGNOSIS: Small cell carcinoma of the lung, clinically limited disease.

PLAN: To be decided.

ca/9-6-XX

Sue B. Fixem, M.D.

Figure 12-7

Consultation Report: Indented Style

CONSULTATION

August 19, 19XX

Manuel Muro, M.D.
1219 Wilson Avenue
Anytown, AS 00004-1219

Re: Franco Sueno

This 30-year-old Mexican male was seen in the neurological clinic at your request. This patient, primarily, has complaints of insecure feelings. Essentially there are no neurological complaints. He has never been unconscious, although once he received a blow on the head. He has had no significant illnesses, none of a neurological nature. A recent lumbar puncture was performed. The cerebrospinal fluid obtained revealed a total protein of 64 mg% and a slight increase in the Pandy.

Physical Examination: Neurological - reveals an alert, cooperative, 30-year-old male. Serial examination of the cranial nerves, two through twelve, reveals no abnormalities or sensory deficits. Fundoscopic examination: within normal limits. No engorgement of the veins. Disks are well outlined, showing no elevation. Motor examination: no lateralizing or focal weakness; no cerebellar signs present. Sensory examination: within normal limits to all modalities tested. Reflex examination: symmetrical, muscle stretch reflexes 1+ to 2+. No pathological reflexes present.

At the present time this patient has a normal neurological examination and no neurologic complaints. I would advise a repeat of the cerebrospinal fluid examination, with accurate pressure measurements simultaneously, being certain that the patient is well relaxed. If the protein remains elevated, repeat the examination again in six weeks.

Robin U. Sharp. M.D.

Figure 12-8

KEY IDEA: OPERATIVE REPORTS

Operative reports contain surgeon's name, patient's name and date, patient number (and room number if inpatient). In order to provide the best care possible, operative reports are dictated immediately following surgery. For the same reason, they should be transcribed and filed on the patient's chart within as short a time as possible, certainly within 24 hours. It will be headed OPERATIVE REPORT, centered or blocked. Both preoperative and postoperative diagnoses will be given, along with the name of the operation and procedure. Each of these headings is usually block format with headings in all capitals, and that particular body format in indented format. The body of the report may be done in one or two paragraphs. The first two lines are indented; the remainder, in block format (see samples, Figures 12-9 and 12-10).

Operative Report: Block Style

```
REPORT OF OPERATION

Citizen, Ima                    Dr. B. A. Uro
#170134

DATE OF OPERATION: 4-26-XX

DATE OF DICTATION: Same.

PREOPERATIVE DIAGNOSIS: R/O obstruction, left
ureter.

POSTOPERATIVE DIAGNOSIS: No evidence of
obstruction, left ureter.

PROCEDURE: Cystourethroscopy with insertion of
left ureteral catheter.

SURGEON: Dr. B. A. Uro

ASSISTANTS: None

ANESTHESIA: General

WHAT WAS DONE: Under adequate inhalation
               anesthesia, the patient was
prepped and draped in the routine sterile manner.
Endoscopic evaluation of the urethra and bladder
showed no intrinsic lesions. The 30- and 70-
degree lens systems were used, and a complete 360-
degree circumferential sweep of the bladder was
done. Both ureteral orifices were identified.
There was no efflux from the right ureteral
orifice. The left orifice was normally positioned
```

and effluxed clear urine. A #6 ureteral catheter was advanced to 25 cm without difficulty. Clear urine followed. Subsequently, the cystoscope was withdrawn. A #16 Foley catheter was inserted and secured to the ureteral catheter. These were then connected to drainage bags. At this point, the patient was repositioned for exploratory laparotomy, which will be dictated by Dr. E. S. Cystic.

ca/4-27-XX

____
Ben A. Uro, M.D.

cc: Dr. E.S. Cystic

Figure 12-9

Operative Report: Indented Style

OPERATIVE REPORT

Iva Weather — Dr. Ben A. Uro
#402140 — Dictated: 10-4-XX

DATE OF PROCEDURE:	10-4-XX
PREOPERATIVE DIAGNOSIS:	Chronic renal disease
POSTOPERATIVE DIAGNOSIS:	Same
OPERATIVE PROCEDURE:	Tenckhoff catheter placement
SURGEON:	Dr. Ben A. Uro
ASSISTANT:	Dr. Robert A. Cutem
ANESTHESIA:	Local with IV Valium

PROCEDURE IN DETAIL: After adequate local anesthesia had been administered, a right infraumbilical paramedian muscle-splitting incision was made, approximately 5 cm long. The skin was opened with a knife down through the subcutaneous tissue. The fascia was then opened sharply and split bluntly. The peritoneum was incised with a small stab blade, and the peritoneal catheter was inserted. After several unsuccessful attempts to place the catheter into the pelvis, it was decided that this would not be possible. A previously placed chromic suture was drawn tight around the Tenckhoff. It was then tacked laterally to the fascia and brought out laterally through a stab incision. The subcutaneous tissue was then closed in the usual manner, and subcuticular stitch was used on the skin. The catheter was observed to work well interoperatively. The patient was returned to her room in good condition.

ca/10-5-XX

____

Ben A. Uro, M.D.

Figure 12-10 Subject lines could be underlined if desired.

In addition to the samples given, an outline format approved by many hospitals is shown in Figures 12-11 and 12-12. Regardless of the formats you learn, you *always* ask for your employer's preference and produce the one that he or she indicates.

HISTORY AND PHYSICAL:

- Your Name - Patient's Name - Medical Records Number (7-digits)
-Chief Complaint.
-Details of present illness including, when appropriate, assessment of patient's emotional, behavioral, and social status.
-Relevant, past social and family history, allergies, medication history.
-Inventory of body segments: HEENT, GI, Cardiovascular, Respiratory, GU, MS, Hematology-Endocrine.

Comprehensive physical exam to include:
General appearance, nutrition, B/P
Head—EENT, mouth, scalp
Neck, thyroid
Lymphadenopathy
Thorax—breasts
Heart and lungs
Abdomen
Pelvic/Genital, Rectal
Extremities
Neurological: Reflexes
Skin
Impression
Plan

Figure 12-11

```
CONSULTATION

Your Name - Patient's Name - Medical Record Number
(7-digits)
Referring Physician
Reason for Consultation
Findings and Recommendations


OPERATIVE REPORT

Your Name - Patient's Name - Medical Record Number
(7-digits)
Preop and Postop Diagnosis
Name of Operation
Description of findings and technical procedure
used and specimens removed if any.


DISCHARGE SUMMARY

Your Name - Patient's Name - Medical Record Number
(7-digits)
Date Admitted, Date Discharged
PRINCIPAL DIAGNOSIS:     condition after study
                         chiefly responsible for
                         admission of patient to
                         hospital.
SECONDARY DIAGNOSIS:     conditions that coexist
                         or develop subsequently at
                         or after time of
                         admission that affect
                         treatment.
Operations performed
Significant findings
Treatment rendered
Condition on discharge
Discharge instruction    (physical activity,
                         medications, diet, and
                         follow-up care)
```

Figure 12-12

KEY IDEA: PATHOLOGY, RADIOLOGY, AND IMAGING REPORTS

The *pathology report* is usually typed because the hospital requires it. All fluid or tissue specimens removed during surgery are sent to the pathologist for examination and confirmation. The pathologist then dictates a report for the patient's chart with a copy sent to the surgeon. That report includes the date, patient's number and/or room number, surgeon's name, specimen submitted and location, a *gross* description, a microscopic description, and a diagnosis. The report is signed by the pathologist. It is usually modified block style. See Figure 12-13.

Pathology Report: Block Style

PATHOLOGY REPORT

SPECIMEN: Gallbladder and stones

BRIEF CLINICAL HISTORY: Chronic cystitis

The specimen was received in formalin and labelled "Gallbladder with stones." It consisted of an opened gallbladder which measures 10.0 cm in length, 6.0 cm in width, and 0.2 cm in thickness. Serosa is gray-pink with focal areas of hemorrhage and fibrous adhesions. Mucosa is gray-white and finely granular. Gallbladder neck and cystic duct contain numerous small calculi, averaging 0.3 cm diameter. Cystic duct measures 3.0 cm in length and 0.8 cm in width. There are numerous grey-yellowish, soft calculi, ranging from 0.3 to 2.0 cm in greatest dimension.

MICROSCOPIC DIAGNOSIS: Chronic cholecystitis with cholelithiasis.

Figure 12-13

Radiology Reports

Radiology reports originate in the x-ray department and are dictated for all imaging procedures. Block and semi-block are most commonly used. Some hospitals have both x-ray and imaging departments, although they may be combined. The traditional x-ray is a film of bones and joints, soft tissue and special studies of internal organs. The special studies require some form of contrast media. See Appendix E for a list of the most common ones. (A complete list of these media are contained in Sloane's *A Word Book in Radiology*.)

Other methods of imaging are *steroscopy* (structures in dimension), *tomography* (structures in layers), *computed axial tomography* (CT scan—a specific slice of any area of the body), *xeroradiography* (x-ray images using dry photocopier), and *sonogram* or *echogram* (diagnostic sound waves), and *magnetic resonance imaging* (MRI—radio frequencies and a range of magnetic field strengths). Reports for all these methods are dictated and transcribed.

Radiotherapy treatment for malignancy is also provided by some facilities. Those treatments are dictated radiotherapy summaries, usually narrative block.

The imaging and x-ray reports (Figures 12-14 and 12-15) include the date, patient's name and number, doctor's name, type of report, and the interpretation and impression of the radiologist. *Nuclear medicine* states the interpretation, impression, and any other pertinent information (Figure 12-16).

X-Ray Report: Block Style

X-RAY & IMAGING, INC.
2400 North Dover, Suite 607
Anytown, AS 00003-2400

ADAMS, Paula J. Dr. Seamly

No. 89-2672 AGE: 45

11-27-XX

X-RAY REPORT

ACUTE ABDOMINAL SERIES:

AP supine and erect views of the abdomen demonstrate a normal bowel gas pattern without evidence of obstructive alteration or adynamic ileus. There is no free air identified. No intra-abdominal calcification is depicted. The properitoneal fat lines are intact. The retroperitoneal structures are grossly normal.

There is a mild levoscoliosis of the lower lumbar spine.

IMPRESSION: Unremarkable abdomen.

CHEST:

There are bibasilar discoid atelectatic strands most pronounced on the left.

Patchy infiltrates involve the upper lung fields more pronounced on the right than the left, and they are fibronodular nature. They appear to be of acute etiology. The pleurodiaphragmatic, osseous, and soft tissue structures are normal.

IMPRESSION: Bibasilar discoid atelectasis

Bilateral upper lobe nonspecific
mixed fibronodular infiltrates
consistent with pneumonitis.

AEG/ca

____

Al E. Gator, M.D.

Figure 12-14

Radiology Report: Modified Block Style

ABC RADIOLOGY DIAGNOSTIC CENTER
2480 North Dover, Suite 206
Anytown, AS 00003-2480
Phone: (014)263-4100

RADIOLOGY REPORT

ABDOMINAL SONOGRAM:

Using a 3.5 mHz transducer, multiple images of the upper abdomen are obtained.

Ultrasonic Murphy's sign was negative. The gallbladder is well distended without evidence of any gallstones. The common bile duct is normally seen and measures 2 mm. No evidence of intrahepatic ductal dilatation is seen.

The liver demonstrates normal homogeneity without evidence of focal masses.

A 6.7 X 4.7 cm sonolucent area is seen adjacent to the head of the pancreas in an inferior and right lateral location. The rest of the head of the pancreas demonstrates normal echogenic pattern.

Both kidneys are normally visualized; the right measures 8.4 cm and left 7.1 cm in the longest dimension.

IMPRESSION: No gallstones seen.

6.7 X 4.7 cm sonolucent mass adjacent to the head of the pancreas in more right lateral and inferior location. The possibilities include lymphadenopathy,

resolving hematoma, from
previous trauma or pancreatic mass.
A CAT scan of the abdomen is
recommended for further evaluation.

Thank you for this referral.

Sylvester Sudz, M.D.

SS:lw
D&T 9-27-XX

Figure 12-15

Nuclear Medicine Report: Block Style

ABC Radiology Diagnostic Center
2480 North Dover, Suite 206
Anytown, AS 00003-2480
Phone: (014)263-4100

RADIOLOGY REPORT

NAME: ADAMS, Paula J. X-RAY NO.: 1168
AGE: 45 ROOM NO.: OP
REFERRED BY: Steve Seamly, M.D. DATE: 12-07-XX

PART EXAMINED: LIMITED CT SCAN OF THE ABDOMEN

This study was performed as a followup examination to an ultrasound of the abdomen performed the same day which demonstrated an enlarged right upper quadrant mass. Initially, the patient was given oral contrast and 10-mm thick images obtained at 20-mm intervals through the liver. At this point, it was determined that the patient had had a previous CT scan at X-Ray Imaging, Inc., about one month previously. Accordingly, it was determined that it was not necessary to repeat the CT at this time; and that in all likelihood, a percutaneous biopsy could be performed pending review of the outside CT scan. Thus at the time the biopsy was performed, a formal CT scan of the abdomen could be completed. That matter was discussed with the patient, who was then referred back to Dr. Steve Seamly's office to discuss performing a percutaneous biopsy at a future date. After discussion with Dr. Seamly, the patient was indeed

```
scheduled for a biopsy on December 8, 19XX.
However, the patient later telephoned to cancel
the CT-directed biopsy.

The images that were obtained demonstrate a very
large mass with its epicenter near the gallbladder
fossa. The mass has the greatest dimension of
approximately 16 cm and consists of a relatively
dense periphery with a low density center. The
gallbladder is not identified separately. The
duodenum and stomach appear deviated towards the
left. No other definite abnormalities are seen.

IMPRESSION:

1.  Large right upper quadrant mass.
    Differential diagnosis includes hepatic
    neoplasm, pancreatic neoplasm, or gallbladder
    carcinoma.

2.  Please see the above discussion as to reasons
    that this examination is not complete and for
    discussion as to reason biopsy has not been
    performed as yet.

Sylvester Sudz, M.D.
SS/ca   12-13-XX
```

Figure 12-16

A list of possible radiology reports and various contrast media used may be found in Appendix E. A nuclear medicine list is also given as a separate part of that appendix.

KEY IDEA: OTHER REPORTS

Medicolegal reports are most often given in connection with personal injury, involving an accident or worker's compensation case. They may originate from either the hospital or medical office, but generally the medical office. The request usually comes from an attorney requesting supportive information for his client. A response should be prompt and complete, with the main element being clarity. Medical secretaries who do transcription may occasionally be asked to help compose the first draft, extracting the following facts from the patient's medical record:

Patient's name, age, date of birth, and address.

Date of the accident or injury and time of day, if known.

History of the accident, injury, or illness in the *patient's own words, if possible.*

Present complaints (subjective complaints) at time of the first visit.

Past history and preexisting conditions.

Physical findings (objective findings) from examination.

Laboratory and radiology findings.

Operative reports, if any.

Consultation notes or opinions.

Diagnosis or diagnoses in detail.

Prescribed treatment given and advised. This should be detailed, listing every visit and treatment, even medications.

Work restrictions and the date for return to work.

Prognosis with estimate of full disability, limitations, and pain.

The report will be addressed to the person or agency requesting the report, should be in letter narrative format, using block or modified block style. It must be signed by the attending physician. The *physician's billing statement* copy, itemized by date and service, will accompany the medicolegal report. Special care should be taken to produce a perfect document in every detail, since it is a legal document and the physician may be required to appear in court.

When a patient dies unexpectedly or under suspicious conditions, either in or out of the hospital, an autopsy may be required to determine the cause of death. This written record may be referred to as an *autopsy protocol*. There are five forms used: (1) the narrative, (2) the numerical, (3) the pictorial (hand drawings), (4) forms based on sentence completion or multiple choice, and (5) the problem-oriented report (based on the Problem-Oriented Medical Handbook). Some include a clinical history. Whichever format is used, the following general guidelines apply:

External Description.

Evidence of injury, either external or internal.

Systems and organs.

Special dissections and examinations.

Brain and other organs after fixation.

Microscopic examinations.

Findings, factual and interpretive (diagnosis).

Opinion, interpretive (conclusion).

Signature.

KEY IDEA CORRECTIONS

In Chapter one it was explained how to handle *corrected reports*. The general rule for making corrections was not covered. Regardless of the type of letter or report, there are specific rules for making corrections.

All types of medical records will occasionally contain errors. In typewritten or word processing work an error discovered immediately can be corrected easily. Using the correction key on the typewriter is extremely simple. A correction key will either cover the error or lift it off the paper. If the typewriter does not have a correction key, there are numerous kinds of correction paper and tape that can be used. Word processing is almost as easy: Corrections are made by deleting the error and replacing it immediately. "White out" should never be used with an electronic typewriter.

Once an entry is an official part of the record the process is quite different. NO PART OF ANY RECORD SHOULD EVER BE DESTROYED OR REPLACED. The correction may be written or typed. The error is crossed through with *one line only.* The word "error," or the abbreviation "corr" should be recorded nearby along with the date. The correction is then made and initialed. All corrections are made in the margins, either left or right, being consistent in all instances.

SUMMARY

In both medical office and hospital, the transcriptionist types numerous medical reports and records. It is of utmost importance that they be accurate. Complete and accurate records and reports are extremely important, because they are legal documents. Formatting these various records and reports may follow the standards, but it is most important to format according to the choice of your employer.

LEARNING ACTIVITIES

ACTIVITY 12-1

A history and physical examination for Ura Payne and Ona Ladder follow. All information on each patient is contained in one run-on paragraph. You are to type each of them in two formats: Ona Ladder should be typed in block and modified block; Ura Payne is to be typed in indented and proper run-on styles.

HISTORY AND PHYSICAL EXAMINATION

Ona Ladder, #350896, Dr. S. Seamly.
DATE OF DICTATION: 10-2-XX. DATE OF ADMISSION: 10-2-XX. DATE OF TRANSCRIPTION: 10-4-XX. REASON FOR ADMISSION: Headaches with nausea and vomiting. CONCISE HISTORY: This 8-year-old male was seen in the office prior to admission with 2-day history of nausea, vomiting, and headache. The child's headaches have been increasing recently in frequency and severity. PAST HISTORY: Essentially negative. No previous serious

illnesses or hospitalization. SYSTEMIC REVIEW: No other recent symptoms are reported. FAMILY HISTORY: Noncontributory. GENERAL APPEARANCE: Well-developed, well-nourished child, alert and oriented. HEENT: Within normal limits. NECK: Supple. No masses. CHEST: Clear to A&P. HEART: Normal sinus rhythm without murmur. ABDOMEN: Scaphoid. LSK within normal limits. Bowel sounds also within normal limits. EXTREMITIES: Normal in appearance. EXTERNAL GENITALIA: Normal in appearance. ADMISSION DIAGNOSIS: Headaches, etiology to be determined. SS/ca Steven Seamly, M.D.

HISTORY AND PHYSICAL EXAMINATION

Ura Payne, #398650, Dr. Goode, Dictated: 11-2-XX. CHIEF COMPLAINT: Frequency and dysuria. PRESENT ILLNESS: This 15-year-old male was seen in the office prior to admission because of recent frequency and dysuria. The patient and his mother gave history that the patient has had, on previous occasions, proteinuria, and has been treated on three previous occasions for urinary tract infection. It was thought advisable to admit the patient for further evaluation due to the recurrence of the problem. PAST MEDICAL HISTORY: Negative except as above. REVIEW OF RECENT SYMPTOMS: Otherwise negative. FAMILY HISTORY: Noncontributory. SOCIAL HISTORY: The patient is a 10th grader. He does well in school. PHYSICAL EXAMINATION: GENERAL APPEARANCE: Well-developed, well-nourished adolescent in no acute distress, alert, cooperative, well oriented. HEENT: No abnormalities. NECK: Supple. No masses. CHEST: Clear to auscultation and percussion. HEART: No murmur heard. ABDOMEN: No organomegaly. Liver, kidneys, and spleen within normal limits. EXTERNAL GENITALIA: Normal. EXTREMITIES: Appear normal. ADMITTING IMPRESSION: Recurrent urinary tract infections. IBG/ca 11-4-XX. I. B. Goode, M. D.

ACTIVITY 12-2

1. How many different formats can be used for history and physical examinations? ______________________

2. Name them: ______________________

____

3. What is the usual style for a radiology report? __________

____

4. In your opinion, why would it be a good idea to type the history and physical on separate pages? ______________

____

5. When is an autopsy report necessary? ______________

____

6. Consultations may originate in two different places. What are they? ______________

____

7. Pathology reports include two types of examination results. Name them. ______________

____

8. What type of patients are most usually involved in medicolegal reports? ______________

____

9. Distinguish between hospital- and physician-originated transcribing by placing an H (hospital) and P (physician) in front of the proper document. Some might need both.

___ History and Physical ___ Pathology Report
___ Operative Report ___ Consultation
___ Progress Notes ___ Prescriptions
___ Radiology Report ___ CT Scan
___ Medicolegal Report ___ Phone Calls

ACTIVITY 12-3

There are two consultations with all information in one run-on paragraph. You are to type the first one concerning Cookie A. Senn in letter narrative, full block. The second one concerning Carla Soong is to be typed letter narrative, modified block, 8-½ × 11-in. paper without letterhead.

Consultation June 19, 19XX, Nguyen P. Tedstrom, Optometrist, 2190 Willhold Avenue, Anytown, AS 00004-1234. Dear Nguyen: Regarding: Cookie A. Senn. Thank you for referring Ms. Senn, whom we saw on June 17, 19XX. As you may recall, she has had blurred vision in the left eye for the past several years. In addition, you are aware that this cannot be improved with lenses. At the present time the visual acuity in the right eye is 20/25, and the left eye is 20/200. There are marked macular degenerative changes noted in the left retina with numerous edema residues. In addition, the left optic disc is very pale. The right retina appears normal. Visual field examination performed revealed a relative central scotoma in the left eye. Tension is 17 mm of mercury Schiotz with a 5.5 gm weight. She was advised that there is no treatment for the diminution of vision in her left eye. Thank you for referring this patient. Cordially, I. Makem See, M.D. IMS:bs

Consultation July 19, 19XX, Richard L. Bordeaux, M.D., 440 Common Street, Anytown, AS 00002-0440. Dear Dick: Regarding: Carla Soong. Thank you for referring Miss Soong, whom we saw on July 15, 19XX. As you will recall, there was some question of muscle imbalance about which the parents were concerned. The child was a product of a full-term normal delivery and has had no known serious injuries. At the present time the eye examination is entirely normal except for prominent epicanthal folds associated with a rather broad nasal bridge. There is no strabismus by Hirschberg or cover tests. The epicanthal folds do, however, at times create the illusion of esotropia. The media and fundi are entirely normal. Her visual acuity is 20/20 in each eye, and there is no refracted error by manifest and cycloplegic refractions. The mother was reassured that there was no ocular problem here, but the child should be rechecked in one year. Thank you for referring this patient. Cordially, I. Makem See, M.D. IMS:bs

ACTIVITY 12-4

Both the operative report and discharge summary are typed in run-on paragraphs, Type them according to the outline in Figure 12-12.

Patient: Emma Joy, #6234510, July 10, 19XX. OPERATIVE REPORT Preoperative Diagnosis: Mandible fracture. Operation Proposed: Extraction of teeth and reduction of mandibular fracture. Anesthesia: Naso-tracheal general anesthesia. Findings: Fractured mandible of the right body extending inferiorly and anteriorly from the second bicuspid - first molar interspace to the inferior border. There were numerous fractured teeth and areas of alveolar process, particularly in the maxillary right quadrant. The following teeth were fractured - the maxillary right central incisor, lateral incisor, first bicuspid, second bicuspid, the first molar, and the lower right first molar, and the lower left first molar. The maxillary right cuspid was avulsed anteriorly but not fractured. The right maxillary alveolar process was comminuted and displaced somewhat toward the palate. Procedure: The patient was prepared and draped for an intraoral procedure. With suction tip and forceps many fragmented teeth were removed, along with numerous bone fragments. The remaining root portions of the maxillary right lateral incisor and first bicuspid were removed. The remaining fractured teeth were left in the alveolar process to aid in stabilization of the fractured mandible. There are numerous pulp exposures on these remaining teeth. Erich arch bars were cut to fit the maxillary and mandibular arches. Gauge #25 stainless steel wires were used to ligate the arch bar to the respective arches. Two #25 gauge stainless steel wires were used to ligate the mobile maxillary right cuspid to the arch bar in an attempt to retain it in its original position. The mandibular fracture was reduced and the mandible was immobilized with four intra-maxillary #25 gauge stainless steel wires. Blood loss: approximately 200 cc. Condition of patient at end of operation: Good. Postoperative diagnosis: Same as preoperative. Operation performed: Same as proposed. bs.

DISCHARGE SUMMARY Patient: Samuel B. Shaw, #4848333, April 16, 19XX. Final Diagnosis: 1. Fracture of the mandible. 2. Multiple lacerations. Procedures: 1. Wiring of the jaw. 2. Repair of lacerations. Disability dates: 3/7/XX to 4/20/XX. History of Present Illness: This 28-year-old Caucasian male was brought to the Emergency Room on 3/7/XX with the chief complaint of difficulty breathing and generalized soreness and pain. The patient had been in an automobile accident at 1 a.m. He had evidently been returning home from a drinking party. Physical examination of the patient in the Emergency Room revealed that the mandible was acutely tender, and the patient had rib tenderness on the right side. The patient also had multiple facial and chest lacerations, which were sutured in the Emergency Room. He was somewhat somnolent and had a fairly ethanol odor on his breath according to the examining physician. Diagnostic Data: Skull series done on 3/7/XX showed no abnormalities except for an oblique fracture seen on the mandible. The ribs showed a number of fractures in the 2nd, 3rd, 5th, 6th, and 7th ribs with some displacement. There was no evidence of trauma to the knee on x-ray. Course in Hospital: Because of the above findings the patient was placed in the hospital and arrangements were made to have his jaw wired by the oral surgeon after his condition had stabilized. The patient had no flail chest or hemothorax; and, therefore, his rib fractures were treated with bed rest. The jaw was wired on 3/9/XX. The patient did well after his surgery and was discharged from this hospital on 3/13/XX. Discharge Program: Patient to be followed by Dr. Bole and Dr. Gunderson in the Outpatient Department. (Signature) Zene Goe, M.D./bs

ACTIVITY 12-5

Type both x-ray reports (Esther Card and Susie Wong) according to the samples given in Figures 12-14 and 12-15.

X-RAY REPORT Esther Card, #142376, March 14, 19XX. PA & Lateral Chest. There is some increase in the pulmonary markings in both bases. There is no evidence of effusion. Expansion is normal. There is a Ghon complex in the left mid-lung field. The cardiac silhouette is normal with no evidence of left ventricular hypertrophy. The arch of the aorta is prominent with a broad appearance in the mediastinum. The bony structures are within normal limits. Impression: Increased pulmonary markings, both bases. No infiltrates and no effusion. No evidence of left ventricular hypertrophy. Redundant aorta. C. Thru, M.D., Radiologist.

X-RAY REPORT Susie Wong, #190673, May 30, 19XX. Dorsal Spine Films of the dorsal spine show slight increase in dorsal kyphosis. There is slight narrowing of the interspaces between D7-8 and 9 with irregularity of the adjacent articular surfaces. This is consistent with an old epiphysitis. No acute injury is evident. Lung fields appear grossly clear. Paraspinal shadows appear normal. There is a small metallic foreign body measuring 3 mm in size lying at the level of the 6th dorsal vertebra in the mid-clavicular line. This is markedly posterior but probably is still within the lung. Impression: 1. Wedging of D7-8 and 9 with irregularity consistent with an old epiphysitis. 2. Small metallic foreign body in the posterior aspect of the left mid-portion of the left lung. C. Thru, M.D., Radiologist bs

ACTIVITY 12-6

Type this run-on pathology report into a proper modified block style.

SURGICAL PATHOLOGY - TISSUE EXAMINATION Patient: Black S. Knight, #2160921, January 23, 19XX. Clinical Data: Age 60 - M - C. Specimen: Mediastinal mass. Description: The specimen is received in three containers: Number 1 is a 10 X 8 X 2 mm, somewhat triangular portion of rather soft, gray tissue. Number 2 consists of several types of tissue. One is a rib which measures 15 X 1.5 X 1 cm. A smaller segment of rib measuring 3 cm in length is also present. Two pieces of blood clot accompany the specimen. Each measures about 3 X 1.5 X 1 cm. Also two pieces of quarter-inch tape are present. Each measures about 20 cm in length. Also present are three pieces of soft, browning tissue. Each measures 1 cm across. Two pieces of fatty tissue each measuring 2 X 1 X 1 cm are present. One contains a portion of suture material attached. The third portion is a nodular mass of firm, rubbery, dark brown tissue measuring 2 X 1.8 X 1 cm. It is said to represent a lymph node. Section shows homogenous light gray, rather glistening surfaces with a rim of hemorrhagic tissue measuring 3 mm in width, partly encircling the mass. Micro: The sections of lymph nodes show metastatic tumor, which is composed of masses of small round or ovoid hyperchromatic cells about a thin, scanty, fibrous stroma. There is some invasion of the fibrofatty tissue also. A section of the biopsy for frozen section appears similar but shows some distortion because of freezing employed. The tissue is consistent with a malignant thymoma. Sections of fibrofatty tissue containing small lymph nodes are also present. These are edematous and hemorrhagic, but show no metastatic tumor. Several fragments of fibrocartilage are present with the specimen. Diagnosis: Malignant thymoma. Case. E. Beer, M.D., Pathologist sb

Bibliography

Blakisten's Gould Medical Dictionary. New York: McGraw-Hill Book Company, 1990.

BRUCE, FLORENCE M., *Medical Transcription Course.* Rye, NY: Dictaphone, Inc., 1983.

BURACK, SYLVIA K., *The Writer's Handbook.* Boston, MA: The Writer, Inc., 1988.

COX, KAY, *Being a Health Unit Coordinator.* Bowie, MD: Robert J. Brady Company, 1984.

Dorland's Illustrated Medical Dictionary, 27th ed. Philadelphia, PA: W. B. Saunders, a Division of Harcourt Brace Jovanovich, Inc., 1988.

FORDNEY, MARILYN, and MARCY DIEHL, *Medical Transcription Guide, Do's and Don'ts.* Philadelphia, PA: W. B. Saunders, a Division of Harcourt Brace Jovanovich, Inc., 1990.

FORDNEY, MARILYN, and MARCY DIEHL, *Medical Typing and Transcribing Techniques and Procedures,* 2nd ed. Philadelphia, PA: W. B. Saunders, a Division of Harcourt Brace Jovanovich, Inc. 1983.

FRANK, MARCELL, *Modern English Exercises for Non-native Speakers, Part II,* 2nd ed. Englewood Cliffs, NJ: Prentice Hall Regents, 1972.

GUTH, HANS P., *Words and Ideas,* 2nd ed. Belmont, CA: Wadsworth Publishing Company, 1966.

KINN, MARY E. *Medical Terminology Building Blocks for Health Careers.* Philadelphia, PA: Delmar Publishers Inc., 1990.

KLEIN, A. E., *Medical Tests and You.* New York: Grosset and Dunlap, 1977.

LEGGETT, GLENN C., DAVID MEAD, and WILLIAM CHARVAT, *Handbook for Writers*, 3rd ed. Englewood Cliffs, NJ: Prentice Hall, 1962.

LEONARD, PEGGY C., *Quick and Easy Medical Terminology.* Philadelphia, PA: W. B. Saunders, a Division of Harcourt Brace Jovanovich, Inc., 1990.

MARSHALL, JACQUELYN, and KATHLEEN HARRIS, *Being a Medical Clerical Worker.* Englewood Cliffs, NJ: Brady, a Prentice Hall Division, 1990.

The Merck Manual, 16th ed. Westpointe, PA: Merck, Sharpe and Dohme Research Laboratories, 1990.

MITCHELL, CAROL A., *Machine Transcription.* Indianapolis, IN: Bobbs-Merrill Educational Publishing, 1983.

PASEWARK, WILLIAM A., *The Gregg Reference Manual*, 6th ed. New York: Gregg Division, McGraw-Hill, Inc., 1985.

ROGET, PETER M., *Roget's International Thesaurus.* New York: Thomas Y. Crowell Company, 1970.

RUDMAN, JACK, *Medical Transcribing Machine Operator.* Syossett, NY: National Learning Corp., 1988.

SABIN, WILLIAM A., *The Gregg Reference Manual*, 6th ed. New York: Gregg Division, McGraw-Hill, Inc., 1985.

SCHORER, MARK, PHILIP DURHAM, and EVERETT L. JONES, *Harbrace College Reader.* New York: Harcourt, Brace, and World, 1959.

SHRODES, CAROLYN, CLIFFORD JOSEPHSON, and JAMES R. WILSON, *Reading for Rhetoric Applications to Writing.* New York: The MacMillan Company, 1965.

SLOANE, SHEILA B., *Medical Abbreviations and Eponyms.* Philadelphia, PA: W. B. Saunders, a Division of Harcourt Brace Jovanovich, Inc., 1985.

SLOANE, SHEILA B., *A Wordbook in Radiology.* Philadelphia, PA: W. B. Saunders, a Division of Harcourt Brace Jovanovich, Inc., 1988.

SOHN, DAVID A., and EDWARD ENGER, *Writing by Doing, Learning to Write Effectively.* Lincolnwood, IL: National Textbook Company, 1985.

Taber's Cyclopedic Dictionary, 16th ed. Philadelphia, PA: F. A. Davis, 1988.

WARDEN-TAMPARO, CAROL D., and MARCIA A. LEWIS, *Diseases of the Human Body.* Philadelphia, PA: F. A. Davis, 1989.

WARRINER, JOHN E., *Warriner's English Grammar and Composition, Fourth Course.* Orlando, FL: Harcourt Brace Jovanovich, Inc., 1982.

Webster's New Collegiate Dictionary, 150th Anniversary Edition. Springfield, MA: G. & C. Merriam Company, 1981.

Webster's New Dictionary of Synonyms. Springfield, MA: G. & C. Merriam Company, 1973.

Webster's New World Secretarial Handbook, 4th ed. New York: Webster's New World, 1989.

Webster's Synonyms, Antonyms, and Homonyms. New York: Barnes and Noble, 1974.

APPENDIX A

Common Word Elements Used In Health Care

Word Element	*Meaning*	*Example*	*Pronunciation*
a-, an-	without, lack of, deficient, absent	asepsis anemia	a/SEP/sis an/E/mia
ab-, abs-	from, away	abnormal abscess	ab/NORM/al ABS/cess
ad-	near, toward	adrenal	ad/REN/al
adeno	gland	adenopathy	ad/en/OP/a/thy
aero	air	anaerobe	an/A/er/obe
alb	white	albuminuria	al/BU/min/ur/i/a
-algia	pain	analgesia	an/al/GE/si/a
ambi-	both	ambidextrous	am/bi/DEX/trous
angio	vessel	angioma	an/gi/O/ma
ano	anus	anoscope	A/no/scope
ante-	before	antenatal	an/te/NAT/al
anti-	against	antiseptic	an/ti/SEP/tic
arterio	artery	arteriosclerosis	ar/ter/i/o/scler/O/sis
arthro	joint	arthroplasty	AR/thro/plas/ty
-asthenia	weakness	myasthenia	my/as/THE/ni/a
auto-	self	autopathy	au/to/PATH/y
bi-	two, twice	bicellular	bi/SEL/u/lar
bio-	life	biology	bi/o/lo/gy
brady-	slow	bradycardia	brad/y/CAR/di/a
broncho	bronchus	bronchitis	bron/CHI/tis
carcino	cancer of epithelial tissue	carcinogen	car/CIN/o/gen

Word Element	Meaning	Example	Pronunciation
cardio	heart	myocardium	my/o/CAR/di/um
-cele	tumor, swelling	enterocele	EN/ter/o/cele
-centesis	puncture	thoracentesis	tho/ra/cen/TE/sis
cephalo	head	hydrocephaly	hy/dro/CEPH/al/y
chole	gall	cholelithiasis	cho/e/lith/I/a/sis
cholecysto	gallbladder	cholecystectomy	cho/le/cys/TECT/o/my
choledocho	common bile duct	choledochostomy	chol/ed/o/CHOS/to/my
chondro	cartilage	chondroma	chon/DRO/ma
-cide	kill	germicide	GERM/i/cide
circum-	around	circumcision	cir/cum/CI/sion
-cise	cut	excise	ex/CISE
colo	colon	colitis	co/LI/tis
colpo	vagina	colporrhaphy	col/POR/rha/phy
contra-	against	contraception	con/tra/CEP/tion
costo	rib	intercostal	in/ter/COS/tal
cranio	skull	craniotomy	cra/ni/OT/o/my
cyano	blue	cyanotic	cy/an/OT/ic
cysto	urinary bladder	cystogram	CYS/to/gram
cyto	cell	monocyte	MON/o/cyte
de-	down, from	decubitus	de/CU/bi/tus
denti	tooth	dentistry	DEN/tis/try
dermo, derma	skin	dermatology	derm/a/TOL/o/gy
dextro	right	dextrocardia	dex/tro/CARD/i/a
di-	two	diplopia	dip/LOP/i/a
dia-	through, between	diarrhea	di/a/RRHE/a
dis-	apart, free of	dissect	dis/SECT
dys-	painful, difficult	dysmenorrhea	dys/men/o/RRHE/a
ecto-	outer	ectocytic	ect/o/SI/tic
-ectomy	surgical removal	prostatectomy	pros/ta/TEC/to/my
-emesis	vomiting	hematemesis	hem/at/EM/e/sis
-emia	blood	leukemia	leu/KE/mi/a
en-	in, inside	encapsulated	en/CAP/su/la/ted
encephalo	brain	encephalitis	en/ceph/a/LI/tis
endo-	within, inner	endometrium	en/do/ME/tri/um
entero	intestine	enteritis	en/ter/I/tis
epi-	above, over	epigastric	ep/i/GAS/tric
erythro	red	erythrocyte	er/yth/RO/cyte
-esthesia	sensation	anesthesia	an/es/THE/si/a
ex-, extra-	out	extrahepatic	ex/tra/HEP/a/tic
febr	fever	afebrile	a/FEB/rile
fibro	connective tissue	fibroma	FI/bro/ma
gastro	stomach	gastrocele	GAS/tro/cele
-gene, -genic	production, origin	neurogenic	neu/ro/GEN/ic
glosso	tongue	glossalgia	glos/SAL/gi/a
gluco, glyco	sugar, sweet	glycosuria	gly/co/SUR/i/a

Word Element	*Meaning*	*Example*	*Pronunciation*
-gram	record	myelogram	MY/e/lo/gram
-graph	machine	encephalograph	en/CEPH/al/o/graph
-graphy	practice, process	ventriculography	ven/tri/cu/LOG/ra/phy
gyne	woman	gynecology	gy/ne/COL/o/gy
hema, hemato, hemo	blood	hematology	hem/at/OL/o/gy
hemi-	half	hemiplegia	hem/i/PLE/gi/a
hepa, hepato	liver	hepatitis	hep/a/TI/tis
herni	rupture	hernioplasty	HER/ni/o/plas/ty
histo	tissue	histology	his/TOL/o/gy
hydro-	water	hydronephrosis	hy/dro/neph/RO/sis
hyper-	over, above, increased	hypertension	hy/per/TEN/sion
hypo-	under, beneath, decreased	hypotension	hy/po/TEN/sion
hyster	uterus	hysterectomy	hys/ter/ECT/o/my
-iasis	condition of	urolithiasis	u/ro/lith/I/as/is
ictero	jaundice	icterogenic	IC/ter/o/gen/ic
ileo	ileum (part of small intestine)	ileitis	il/e/I/tis
ilio	ilium (bone)	iliosacrum	il/i/o/SA/crum
inter-, intra-	within	intramuscular	in/tra/MUS/cu/lar
-itis	inflammation of	appendicitis	ap/pen/di/CI/tis
laparo	abdomen	laparotomy	la/par/OT/o/my
-lepsy	seizure, convulse	narcolepsy	NAR/co/lep/sy
leuko	white	leukorrhea	leu/ko/RRHE/a
lipo	fat	lipoma	lip/O/ma
lith	stone	lithocystotomy	lith/o/cys/TOT/o/my
-lysis	loosen, dissolve	hemolysis	hem/OL/y/sis
macro-	large, long	macrocyte	MAC/ro/cyte
mal-	bad, poor	malabsorption	mal/ab/SORP/tion
-mania	insanity	kleptomania	klep/to/MAN/i/a
mast	breast	mastectomy	mas/TEC/to/my
mega-	large	splenomegaly	splen/o/MEG/a/ly
men	month	menstruation	men/stru/A/tion
meso-	middle	mesocardia	mes/o/CAR/di/a
-meter	measure	thermometer	ther/MOM/e/ter
metro	uterus	metrorrhagia	met/ror/RHA/gia
micro-	small	microscope	MIC/ro/scope
mono-	single, one	monocyte	MON/o/cyte
muco	mucous membrane	mucocutaneous	mu/co/cu/TA/ne/ous
myco	fungus	mycosis	my/CO/sis
myelo	spinal cord, bone marrow	myelomeningocele	my/el/o/men/IN/go/cele
myo	muscle	myopathy	my/OP/a/thy
narco	stupor	narcotic	nar/COT/ic

Word Element	*Meaning*	*Example*	*Pronunciation*
naso	nose	nasopharynx	nas/o/PHA/rynx
natal	birth	prenatal	pre/NA/tal
necro	death	necropsy	NEC/rop/sy
neo-	new	neoplasm	NE/o/plasm
nephro	kidney	nephritis	ne/PHRI/tis
neuro	nerve	neuralgia	neu/RAL/gi/a
non-	no, not	nontoxic	non/TOX/ic
oculo	eye	oculomycosis	OC/u/lo/my/CO/sis
-ology	study of	bacteriology	bac/ter/i/OL/o/gy
-oma	tumor	carcinoma	car/ci/NO/ma
oophor	ovary	oophorectomy	o/opho/REC/to/my
ophthalmo	eye	ophthalmoscope	oph/THAL/mo/scope
-opia	vision	photopic	pho/TOP/ic
-opsy	study of	autopsy	au/TOP/sy
orchi	testicle	orchipexy	ORCH/i/pex/y
-orrhaphy	to repair a defect, suture	herniorrhaphy	her/ni/OR/raph/y
ortho-	straight	orthopedics	orth/o/PED/ics
-oscopy	look into, see	esophagoscopy	e/soph/a/GOS/co/py
-osis	condition of	neurosis	neu/RO/sis
osteo	bone	osteoma	os/te/O/ma
-ostomy	surgical opening	colostomy	col/OST/o/my
oto	ear	otolith	OT/o/lith
-otomy	incision	gastrotomy	gas/TROT/o/my
para-	alongside, abnormal	paraplegia	par/a/PLE/gi/a
path	disease	pathology	pa/THOL/o/gy
ped (Latin)	foot	pedograph	PED/o/graph
ped (Greek)	child	pediatrics	pe/di/AT/rics
-penia	too few, decrease of	leukopenia	leu/ko/PEN/i/a
peri-	around, covering	pericarditis	pe/ri/car/DI/tis
-pexy	to sew up in position	nephropexy	NEPH/ro/pex/y
pharyngo	throat	pharyngoplasty	pha/RYN/go/plas/ty
phlebo	veins	phlebitis	phle/BI/tis
-phobia	fear, dread	photophobia	pho/to/PHO/bi/a
-photo	light	photolysis	pho/TOL/ys/is
-plasty	operative revision	rhinoplasty	RHI/no/plas/ty
-pnea	breathing	orthopnea	or/thop/NE/a
pneumo	air, lungs	pneumonia	pneu/MO/ni/a
poly-	much, many	polyuria	po/ly/U/ri/a
post-	after	postpartum	post/PAR/tum
procto	rectum	proctoscopy	proc/TOS/co/py
pre-	before	preoperative	pre/OP/er/a/tive
-ptosis	falling	nephroptosis	neph/rop/TO/sis
pyelo	pelvis of the kidney	pyelonephritis	py/el/o/neph/RI/tis
pyo	pus	pyogenic	py/o/GEN/ic

Word Element	*Meaning*	*Example*	*Pronunciation*
pyro	heat, temperature	pyrexia	py/REX/i/a
renal	kidney	suprarenal	su/pra/RE/nal
retro-	behind, backward	retrosternal	ret/ro/STER/nal
-rhage	hemorrhage, flow	hemorrhage	HEM/or/rhage
-rhea	flow	diarrhea	di/a/RRHE/a
rhino	nose	rhinopathy	rhi/NOP/a/thy
salpingo	oviduct	salpingectomy	sal/pin/GEC/to/my
sclero	hardening	scleroderma	scle/ro/DER/ma
semi-	half	semicircular	sem/i/CIR/cu/lar
septic	poison, infection	septicemia	sep/ti/CEM/i/a
spleno	spleen	splenocele	SPLE/no/cele
stomato	mouth	stomatitis	sto/ma/TI/tis
sub-	under	subacute	sub/a/CUTE
-therapy	treatment	hydrotherapy	hy/dro/THER/a/py
-thermy	heat	diathermy	DI/a/therm/y
thoraco	chest	thoracotomy	thor/a/COT/o/my
thrombo	clot	thrombosis	throm/BO/sis
thyro	thyroid gland	thyroxin	thy/ROX/in
trans-	across	transfusion	trans/FU/sion
uro	urine	uremia	u/RE/mi/a
-uria, -uric	condition of, presence in urine	uremia	u/RE/mi/a
uni	one	unicellular	u/ni/CELL/u/lar
vaso	blood vessel	vasoconstriction	vas/o/con/STRIC/tion

APPENDIX B

Medical Abbreviations and Symbols

Abbreviation	*Meaning*
ac	before meals
ad	add
ad lib	as desired
Adm.	admission
AIDS	acquired immune deficiency syndrome
AKA	also known as
AMA	American Medical Association
amb.	ambulatory
ant.	anterior
AP	anteroposterior
AP&L	anterior, posterior, and lateral
aqua	water; H_2O
ASAP	as soon as possible
ASHD	arteriosclerotic heart disease
BID	twice a day
BM	bowel movement
BMR	basic metabolic rate
B/P, BP	blood pressure
BR	bed rest
BRP	bathroom privileges
BS	blood sugar
C.	centigrade, Celcius
c̄	with

Abbreviation	*Meaning*
Ca	calcium
ca	cancer
cap	capsule
cath	catheter or catheterization
CAT scan, CT scan	computerized axial tomography scan
CBC	complete blood count
CBR	complete bed rest
cc	cubic centimeter
CCU	coronary care unit
CHF	congestive heart failure
chr	chronic
cm	centimeter
CNS	central nervous system
C/O	complains of
compd	compound
cont	continuous
COPD	chronic obstructive pulmonary disease
CPR	cardiopulmonary resuscitation
CVA	cardiovascular accident
D	dose
DAT	diet as tolerated
dc	discontinue
D/c, DC	discharge
D&C	dilation and curettage
Dim	half
dist	distilled
DNA	does not apply
DOA	dead on arrival
dr	dram
DRG	diagnosis related group
drsg	dressing
D/S	dextrose and normal saline
D/W	dextrose and water
DX, Dx	diagnosis
E	enema
ea	each
ECG, EKG	electrocardiogram
EEG	electroencephalogram
emul	emulsion
ENT	ear, nose, and throat
ER	emergency room
esp	especially
et	and
etiol	etiology

Abbreviation	*Meaning*
FBS	fasting blood sugar
Fe	iron
FF	forced feeding or forced fluids
FH	family history
fld	fluid
FUO	fever of undetermined origin
fx.	fracture
g	grain
GB	gallbladder
GI	gastrointestinal
GM	gram
gt (gtt)	drop (drops)
GTT	glucose tolerance test
GU	genitourinary
gyn	gynecology
HA	headache
HBD	has been drinking
HBP	high blood pressure
Hgb	hemoglobin
H&P	history and physical
hs	bedtime
HSV	herpes simplex virus
HX	history
hyper	above or high
hypo	below or low
ICU	intensive care unit
IM	intramuscular
int.	internal
I&O	intake and output
irrig	irrigation
isol	isolation
IV	intravenous
IVP	intravenous pyelogram
IVPB	intravenous piggyback
K+	potassium
KUB	kidney, ureter, bladder
L. or l	liter
liq	liquid
LLQ	left lower quadrant
LLX	lower left extremities
LP.	lumbar puncture
L.P.N.	Licensed Practical Nurse
Lt.	left
LUQ	left upper quadrant
LVN	Licensed Vocational Nurse

Abbreviation	*Meaning*
mcg	microgram
MD	Doctor of Medicine
med	medicine
meq	milliequivalents
mg	milligram
MI	myocardial infarction
ml	milliliter
mm	millimeter
mn or MN	midnight
MRI	magnetic resonance imaging
Na	sodium
NA	Nursing Assistant
neg	negative
NGT	nasogastric tube
NKA	no known allergies
NPO	nothing by mouth
NS	normal saline
OB/GYN	obstetrics/gynecology
occ.	occasionally
od	right eye
OD	overdose
OP	outpatient
OR	operating room
Ortho	orthopedics
os	left eye
OT	occupational therapy
ou	both eyes
oz	ounce
PAP	Papanicolaou smear
Path.	pathology
pc	after meals
Peds.	pediatrics
per	by, through
PID	pelvic inflammatory disease
PKU	phenylketonuria
PO	by mouth
post	after
post	posterior
post-op	postoperative
PP	postprandial
pre-op	before surgery
prep	preparation
PRN	as needed
prog	prognosis
pt	patient

Abbreviation	*Meaning*
PTA	prior to admission
q	every
qAM	every morning
qd	every day
qh	every hour
qid	four times a day
qod	every other day
qs	quantity sufficient
qt	quart
RLQ	right lower quadrant
RN	Registered Nurse
R/O	rule out
ROM	range of motion
RR	recovery room
RT	respiratory therapist, registered therapist
RUQ	right upper quadrant
RX	prescription
s	without
sc	subcutaneous
sign	directions
sol	solution
spec	specimen
ss	half
staph	staphylococcus
stat	immediately
STD	sexually transmitted disease
syr	syrup
T.	temperature
T&A	tonsillectomy and adenoidectomy
Tab	tablet
TAH	total abdominal hysterectomy
T&CM	type and cross-match
THR	total hip replacement
TIA	transient ischemic attack
tid	three times a day
tinc	tincture
TKO	to keep open
TPR	temperature, pulse, respiration
Trx	traction
TUR	transurethral resection
TURP	transurethral resection prostate
TV	tidal volume
Tx	treatment
U	unit

Abbreviation	*Meaning*
UA	urinalysis
UCR	usual, customary, and reasonable
uncon	unconscious
ung	ointment
URI	upper respiratory infection
UTI	urinary tract infection
VD	venereal disease
vs.	vital signs
w/a	while awake
w/b	weight bearing
WBC	white blood count
wc	wheelchair
wt	weight

APPENDIX C

Prescription Abbreviations and Symbols

Periods are no longer considered necessary in prescription abbreviations but it is not *incorrect* to use them if you wish.

Abbreviation	*Meaning*
a.c.	before meals
ad lib.	as much as needed
agit.	shake; stir
ante	before
aq.	water
b.i.d.	two times a day
c	with
caps.	capsule
comp	compound
contra	against
dil.	dilute
dos.	doses
dr.	dram
elix.	elixer
emul.	emulsion
et	and
fl.	fluid
garg.	gargle
Gm.	gram
gr.	grain

Abbreviation	*Meaning*
gt.	drop
gtt.	drops
h.	hour
h.s.	before bedtime
inj.	injection
kg.	kilogram
m	minum
M. or m.	mix
mg.	milligram
ml	milliliter
noct.	night
oz.	ounce
p.c.	after meals
pil.	pill
p.r.n.	whenever necessary
pulv., pwd	powder
q.	every
q. am	every morning
q.d.	one time daily
q. 4 h.	every four hours
q.h.	every hour
q.i.d.	four times a day
q. noc.	every night
q.n.s.	quantity not sufficient
q.o.d.	every other day
q. pm	every night
q.s.	quantity sufficient
Rx	take (recipe), treatment
rep	let it be repeated
s	without
sat.	saturated
sig.	write on label
sol.	solution
s.o.s.	may be repeated once if necessary
ss	one half
stat.	immediately
suppos., supp	suppository
tab.	tablet
t.i.d.	three times a day
tinct.	tincture
troc.	lozenge
u.	unit
5", 10"	5 minutes, 10 minutes
5', 10'	5 hours, 10 hours

APPENDIX D

Two-Letter State Abbreviations

Alabama	AL	Kansas	KS	Ohio	OH
Alaska	AK	Kentucky	KY	Oklahoma	OK
American Samoa	AS	Louisiana	LA	Oregon	OR
Arizona	AZ	Maine	ME	Pennsylvania	PA
Arkansas	AR	Maryland	MD	Puerto Rico	PR
California	CA	Massachusetts	MA	Rhode Island	RI
Canal Zone	CZ	Michigan	MI	South Carolina	SC
Colorado	CO	Minnesota	MN	South Dakota	SD
Connecticut	CT	Mississippi	MS	Tennessee	TN
Delaware	DE	Missouri	MO	Texas	TX
District of Columbia	DC	Montana	MT	Trust Territory	TT
Florida	FL	Nebraska	NE	Utah	UT
Georgia	GA	Nevada	NV	Vermont	VT
Guam	GU	New Hampshire	NH	Virginia	VA
Hawaii	HI	New Jersey	NJ	Virgin Islands	VI
Idaho	ID	New Mexico	NM	Washington	WA
Illinois	IL	New York	NY	West Virginia	WV
Indiana	IN	North Carolina	NC	Wisconsin	WI
Iowa	IA	North Dakota	ND	Wyoming	WY

APPENDIX E

List of Terms Used in Radiology and Related Reports

These are radiology terms that you may encounter in transcribing. In addition to the standard radiologic examinations of the skeletal system, many special examinations are performed. Nuclear medicine and therapy are included.

angiocardiogram
angiogram
aortagram
arteriogram
arthrogram
barium enema
bone density
bone marrow imaging
cardiac blood pool imaging
cardioangiogram
cephalogram
cholangiogram
cholecystogram
cisternogram
computerized axial tomogram (CT scan)
corpora cavernosogram
cystogram
dacryocystogram
diskogram
duodenogram
echocardiogram
echoencephalogram
echogram
encephalogram
endoscopic catheterization
esophogram
fluoroscopy (chest, colon, gallbladder, stomach)
hyperthermia
hysterosalpingogram
imaging: brain, pulmonary, kidney, etc.
imaging: brain scan, Doppler, or real-time scan
intracavity radio-element application
intrastitial radio-element application
intravenous cholangiogram (IVC)
intravenous pyelogram (IVP)
laminagram
laryngogram
lymphangiogram
magnetic resonance imaging (MRI)
mammogram
myelogram, spinal

nephrotomogram
orthopantogram
pelvimetry
perineogram
plasma volume
platelet survival
pneumoencephalogram
radionuclide localization of tumor
radionuclide therapy
red cell volume, determination
retrograde pyelogram (RP)
scan (blood and heart, bone, full body, brain, liver, lung, spleen, thyroid)
sonogram
sialogram
splenoportogram
stereoscopy
teletherapy
therapeutic radiation
thermogram
tomogram
tomographic (SPECT)
transhepatic portogram
ultrasonogram (bile ducts, gallbladder, kidneys, liver, ovaries, uterus)
uptake for endocrine system
urethrocystogram
urogram
vasogram
venogram
ventriculogram
vitamin absorption
white blood cell localization
whole blood volume determination
xeromammogram
xeroradiogram

Contrast Media

Abrodil
acetrizoate
acetrizoic acid
amidotrizoic acid
Amipaque
Angioconray
Angiografin
Angiovist
barium sulfate
benzoic acid
Biligrafin
Biligram
Biliodyl
Bilivistan
Bilopaque
Biloptin
bismuth
Bracco
brominized oil
bunamiodyl
calcium
Cardio-Conray
Cardiografin
cerium
Cholebrine
Chografin
Cholovue
Clysodast
Conray
Cystografin
Cystokon
diaginol
diatrizoate
diatrizoic acid
diodine
diodone
Diodrast
Dionosil
Diprotrizoate
Duografin
Duroliopaque
dysprosium
Endobile
Endografin
Ethiodane
ethiodized oil
Ethiodol
Ethyliodophenylundecyl
gadolinium
Gastrografin
glucagon
Hexabrix
Hippuran
Hypaque
Hytrast
Intropaque
iobenzamic acid
iobutoic acid
iocarmate meglumine
iocarmic acid

iocetamate
iocetamic acid
iodamic acid
iodamide
iodatol
iodecol
iodide
iodipamide
iodized oil
iodolaphionic acid
iodohippurate
iodomethamate
iodophendylate
iodophthalein
iodopyracet
iodoxamate
iodoxamic acid
iodoxyl
ioglicate
ioglicic acid
ioglucol
ioglucomide
ioglunide
ioglycamic acid
ioglycamide
iogulamide
iohexol
iomide
iopamidol
iopanoate
iopanoic acid
iophendylate
iophenoxic acid
ioprocemic acid
iopromide
iopronic acid
iopydol
iopydone
iosefamate
iosefamic acid
ioseric acid
iosulamide
iosumetric acid
iotasul
ioteric acid
iothalamate
iothalamic acid
iotrol
iotroxamide
iotroxic acid
ioxaglate
ioxaglic acid
ioxithalamate
ioxithalamic acid
iozomic acid
ipodate
ipodic acid
Isopaque
Isovue
Kinevac
Lipiodol
Liquapake
magnesium
manganese chloride
meglumine
methiodal
methylglucamine
metrizamide
metrizoate
metrizoic acid
Micropaque
Microtrast
Monophen
Myodil
Neo-Iopax
Niopam
Novopaque
Nyegaard
Omnipaque
Orabilex
Oragrafin
Oravue
Osbil
Pantopaque
phenobutiodyl
phenetetiothalein
potassium bromide
Praestholm
Priodax
propyliodone
Raybar 75
Rayvist
Renografin
Reno-M-30
Reno-M-60
Reno-M-Dip
Renovist
Renovue
Retro-Conray
Salpix
sincalide
Sinografin
Skiodan
Skiodan Acacia
sodium
Solu-Biloptin

Solutrast
Steripaque-BR
Steripaque-V
Telebrix
Telepaque
Teridax
tetrabromophenolphthalein
tetraiodophenolphthalein
Thixokon
thorium dioxide
thorium tartrate
Thorotrast
triiodobenzoic acid
Triosil
tyropanoate
tyropanoic acid
Umbradil
Urografin
Uromiro
Uropac
Urovision
Vasiodone

Index